WAFFEN-SS

THE UNPUBLISHED PHOTOGRAPHS
1923-1945

WAFFEN-SS

THE UNPUBLISHED PHOTOGRAPHS

1923-1945

Christopher Ailsby

MBI Publishing Company

This edition first published in 1998 by
MBI Publishing Company,
729 Prospect Avenue, PO Box 1, Osceola,
WI 54020 USA

Library in Congress Cataloging-in-Publication Data available

ISBN 0-7603-0564-1

Editorial and design by
Brown Packaging Books Ltd
Bradley's Close
74–77 White Lion Street
London N1 9PF

Editor: Peter Darman
Design: Wilson Design Associates
Picture Research: Christopher Ailsby

Printed in Singapore

Many thanks to Roger Hansford for his help

Previous pages: *Totenkopf* soldiers in France, May 1940.

Contents

Introduction

This book is a unique pictorial record of the development of what is probably the most infamous military organisation of the twentieth century: the Waffen-SS (the armed SS). The organisation of the SS as a whole, and its military units in particular, is of course inexorably bound up with the rise of Adolf Hitler and his Nazi Party. Starting out as a small, select group of toughs who protected Hitler and his cronies from enemies during political meetings in Germany in the 1920s, the armed SS grew into an army numbering nearly one million men by the end of World War II.

The Waffen-SS was a part of the SS, being essentially its paramilitary and then military wing, and during the 1920s and 1930s it was strictly controlled by the leader of the SS, Reichsführer-SS Heinrich Himmler. It was always the intention of both Himmler and Hitler that the armed units of the SS would be made up of political warriors, a racial and military élite indoctrinated in National Socialist ideology. To this end recruitment was strictly controlled: only the Third Reich's racially and physically finest were accepted into the Black Corps. This was particularly true of Hitler's bodyguard unit, the *Leibstandarte* under its charismatic commander, 'Sepp' Dietrich. Those recruits who were accepted into the armed SS received ideological indoctrination in the tenets of National Socialism, which left them in no doubt that they were the standard bearers of Nazism in all its forms. Hand-in-hand with this ideological indoctrination went rigorous military training. The training programme devised by Felix Steiner and Paul Hausser produced SS soldiers who were both fit and familiar with the theories of mobile warfare. Unlike in the army there were no social divisions between officers and men: units were trained to operate as teams, each man, regardless of rank, was dependent on his comrade – in this way the Waffen-SS developed a unique camaraderie.

As a consequence of the training, recruitment criteria and indoctrination, by 1939 the armed SS was a small, highly trained and generally well equipped formation, ready for action. Compared to the German Army it was insignificant, and Hitler would have won his campaigns in Poland, the Low Countries, France, Yugoslavia and Greece without Himmler's troops. However, during the string of German victories in 1939-41 the SS fought courageously, and with an *élan* rarely seen among army units. Such conduct won the admiration of both Hitler and Himmler, and the grudging respect of the army (though senior army commanders were disdainful of the reckless courage which often resulted in high SS casualties).

A large proportion of the chapters in this book concern the war on the Eastern Front. This is as it should be, for the war in Russia ultimately decided the fate of the Third Reich and the Waffen-SS. But, more importantly, it was on the Eastern Front that the Waffen-SS won its spurs, becoming, in the eyes of the German Army and the German High Command, a valued military force. If the army had looked aghast at the recklessness of Waffen-SS officers and men in the attack during the years of victory in 1939-41, incurring as it did high casualties, it was grateful indeed for the SS's tenacity and fanaticism in the defence in Russia following the petering out of Operation 'Barbarossa' at the end of 1941.

The war in Russia was important with regard to the development of the Waffen-SS for a number of reason. In many ways the war in the East was the task that the Waffen-SS was created for: a struggle of ideologies – National Socialism versus Bolshevism – in which the soldiers who wore SS runes were in the ideological van. Such an ideological struggle is invariably unrestrained and savage, and so during the war on the Eastern Front the unique fighting qualities of the Waffen-SS, a blend of ideological conviction, courage, recklessness, blind obedience and nihilism, became highly prized among SS and army commanders alike. The furnace of the Eastern Front tempered the élite units of the Himmler's legions, turning them into probably the finest fighting formations in Hitler's armoury. The honour titles of these divisions – *Leibstandarte, Das Reich, Totenkopf, Wiking, Frundsberg* and *Hohenstaufen* – and their greatest actions – Demyansk, Kharkov, Kursk and Cherkassy – have rightly entered military folklore.

In Russia, while army units withdrew or disintegrated in the face of Red Army offensives, the Waffen-SS stood firm. And though SS divisions were often bled white in their attempts to obey their Führer's orders to hold ground, Hitler only saw his SS legions turn seemingly inevitable defeat into victory. In his eyes this was the manifestation of the superiority of National Socialist ideology: that no matter how many divisions the Russians threw at them, the political warriors of the Waffen-SS would eventually triumph. The truth was different, of course, and in the end Hitler would turn on the Waffen-SS in spiteful fury when even it could not fulfil his wishes, but in 1942-43 the Führer began to dream of whole SS armies, which in his opinion would guarantee him ultimate victory in the East.

If Hitler's dreams were firmly rooted in fantasy with regard to the military situation on the Eastern Front after 1942, the tangible results of his mental aberrations were that the Waffen-SS began to receive the best weapons and equipment. Its panzer divisions were liberally equipped with Panther and Tiger Tanks, while Waffen-SS infantry were given armoured personnel carriers to transport them into battle. By mid-1943 the SS panzer divisions were probably the finest military units the Third Reich possessed, and during the last two years of he war had a major strategic impact on both Western and Eastern Fronts.

Parallel to the strengthening of the best Waffen-SS divisions was a rapid expansion in the total number of SS divisions. The war in Russia witnessed a spectacular growth of Himmler's army, but the necessities of war had watered down the racial entry standards so much that they had become meaningless. Tens of thousands of non-German nationals, even from races that the Nazis had previously considered to be 'sub-human', were recruited into the SS in an effort to stave off defeat.

To put together a pictorial record of such a large and diverse organisation as the Waffen-SS necessarily presents problems, and the choice of what to include and what to leave out is a difficult one. However, the unique nature of Christopher Ailsby's photographic library has made the task somewhat easier, though no less daunting. Christopher Ailsby is not only a writer and expert on many aspects of the Third Reich, he is also a collector of its memorabilia. Part of his collection extends to photographs of the period, and not just Waffen-SS. Over many years he has built up a unique photographic library that contains images of all aspects of Germany and German life in the first half of the twentieth century. These images include photographs from the personal albums of individuals who lived through this traumatic period, which give a unique view of the great events that shaped the lives of ordinary people. In addition, the vast majority of the photographs in the book have never been published before, thus creating an unsurpassed illustrated history of the Waffen-SS.

This book of course contains images of the higher SS leaders, such as Heinrich Himmler, 'Sepp' Dietrich and Theodore Eicke, for to omit them would lessen the authority of the work, but it is the images of the ordinary Waffen-SS soldier that makes this book distinctive. These pictures are not only interesting, they also remind the reader that it was the common soldier who participated in the blistering Blitzkrieg campaigns during the first two years of the war, who endured the horrors of the Eastern Front, and who paid the ultimate price in the defence of the Fatherland and National Socialism.

What of the charge that titles such as this glorify the Waffen-SS? While it is true that there is a kind of sinister glamour that has attached itself to the Waffen-SS, the question of indoctrination in National Socialist ideology and the atrocities that ensued as a result of this has been addressed in full in the following pages. That said, while it is true that terrible crimes were committed by troops wearing SS runes, it is also true that thousands of Waffen-SS soldiers never perpetuated atrocities against opposition soldiers or innocent civilians. And it is also important to differentiate between the Waffen-SS and the SS as a whole. This is not to whitewash the whole Waffen-SS, far from it, but to present a balanced and accurate picture of Hitler's Praetorian Guard, which Christopher Ailsby has certainly done.

Peter Darman
Editor

CHAPTER ONE

The Führer's Bodyguard

The early days of the armed SS

The SS grew out of the conditions that ensued following Germany's defeat in World War I. The political intrigues that spawned the Nazi Party and brought about the rise of Adolf Hitler to an unprecedented position of power can only be understood by an examination of the political aftermath that arose after Germany's surrender. The amalgamation of fringe political parties with ex-soldiers' associations – Freikorps – which were roaming aimlessly around Germany in search of stability, combined with the unstable internal situation in Germany, created an environment in which extremists could prosper.

LEFT: Freikorps members on the streets of Berlin in January 1919. Tough and ruthless, many ex-Freikorps men later joined the ranks of the SA and SS.

OPPOSITE: Adolf Hitler, leader of the Nazi Party, whose desire to create a totally loyal bodyguard led to the creation of the SS in 1925.

GERMANY — THE POLITICAL BATTLEGROUND

World War I ended on 11 November 1918, when the Monarchy had been forced to abdicate. Two days later Ludwig III, King of Bavaria, formally signed his abdication and released all Bavarian troops, including Hitler, from their oath of allegiance. This was followed on 28 November by Kaiser Wilhelm II, who then went into exile. This led to a political vacuum that was filled either by the far right or the far left, leaving Germany in chaos and revolt under the frail Weimar Republic. The new republic's army, the Reichswehr, decided to defend itself against subversion. The Bavarian socialist government in Munich, for example, was crushed by central government troops with the aid of their Freikorps allies.

Onto the political stage during this period strode two luminaries, both of whom Hitler was to eventually eclipse. The first was a railway locksmith, Anton Drexler, a harmless-looking, bespectacled man who worked with the Fatherland Party during and after World War I, and whose aim was to get a fair peace for Germany. Drexler merged two tiny groups of malcontents into the Deutsche Arbeiterpartei (DAP), the German Workers' Party, in January 1919. It was an organisation with no assets except a cigar box to hold contributions.

HITLER AND RÖHM

The second, Ernst Röhm, was a far more sinister character: a short, overweight individual with bullet-scarred cheeks. A non-conformist, lecher, homosexual and adventurer, he detested bourgeois normality and felt himself compelled to exploit the chaos which engulfed Germany after her defeat. He had remained in the army after the war and fought in General Ritter von Epp's Freikorps which crushed the Bavarian socialist government. He was also at this time secretly employed by the army to establish ammunition and weapons dumps in the Munich region for the use of monarchist and nationalist groups, and to organise a special political intelligence unit for the army. Adolf Hitler, still a corporal awaiting his discharge from service, was selected for training in this new unit as an education officer in February 1919.

Hitler had deeply held nationalistic views and anti-Semitic prejudices, both of which were bolstered by the political instruction he received during his training. In September, his army intelligence masters sent him to investigate the DAP.

THE RISE OF HITLER

Drexler's ideas appealed to Hitler, as he was bitterly opposed to the 'capitalist Jews' and 'the Marxist conspiracy'. These ideas were later to form the very core of Nazi idealism. For his part Drexler described Hitler as 'an absurd little man'. Hitler manipulated the membership figures to inflate its size and importance, and soon Drexler's position in the party was under threat from Hitler's forceful personality and his persuasive oratory. In less than a year the 'absurd little man' had become the dominant force in the party. Soon afterwards Hitler merged the DAP with the Nationalsozialistische Deutsche Arbeiter Partei (NSDAP), the National Socialist German Workers' Party.

It was at this time that Ernst Röhm chose to support Hitler, thus helping the fledgling Nazi Party to grow. Röhm was chief of staff to the commandant of the Munich military region, and had heady ambitions of forming a revolutionary army with himself as its leader. His chosen vehicle was the secretly armed Bavarian Home Guard. However, the Berlin government, sensing revolution in the air, disbanded this and other military groups which were covertly gathering in various districts of Germany in early 1921. Röhm's ambitions were thus thwarted, but Hitler's embryonic Nazi Party offered him another chance. He believed he could mould Hitler to his own desires and thus usurp his powers, and so began to increase his influence with the party's leader by introducing him to influential persons such as General Erich Ludendorff and General Franz Ritter von Epp. These introductions subsequently bore fruit in giving credibility to Hitler and his party, and financial help soon began to materialise. Money is power and Hitler always appreciated this. He now needed to improve the party's programme, and its visual aspect seemed the best way to do this. German menfolk were accustomed to uniforms and military life and the pageantry that went with it. What better than to harness this militarism with patriotism, both of which had been tempered in the white heat of World War I? For his symbol he chose the female form of the ancient swastika emblem, which on the Nazi flag appeared as 'something akin to a blazing torch'.

THE LEADER'S 'WOLVES'

In the early days of Nazism, Hitler was surrounded by the unwieldy Sturmabteilung (SA) – Brownshirts – tough, unemployed ex-soldiers who frequented Munich beer halls such as the Torbräukeller near the Isar Gate, and who were recruited by Röhm to protect Nazi speakers at public meetings. With growing financial support and a visual political message, Hitler felt able to flex his new-found power, but required a serious confrontation with his political enemies to reinforce his position. This occurred on 4 November 1921, when the social democrats and communists tried to crush his party at the Hoffbrauhaus. As he later somewhat poetically described the event: 'The dance had not yet begun when my storm troopers, for so they were called from this day on, attacked like wolves. They flung themselves in packs of eight or 10 again and again on their enemies, and little by little actually began to thrash them out of the hall. After five minutes, I hardly saw one of them who was not covered with blood. Then two pistol shots rang out and now a wild din of shouting broke out from all sides. One's heart almost rejoiced at this spectacle which recalled memories of the war.'

LEFT: Sturmführer Horst Wessel leads his men through the streets of Nuremberg, 1929. Wessel was shot by communists on 14 January 1930, dying of his wounds nine days later. He was given a martyr's funeral, and the marching song he wrote, *Die Fahne Hoch!*, became the anthem of the Nazi Party.

Late in 1921, at a meeting of the separatist Bavarian Association, Hitler ordered his storm troopers to rush the platform. The fight that ensued ended the meeting. Hitler was subsequently arrested and sentenced to three months' imprisonment (though he only served one month) in the spring of 1922. It was during this time that he and his supporters realised the need for something more spectacular than a beer hall brawl to advance their political standing.

HITLER'S BODYGUARD

The Brownshirts were to expand in number, but they acted under Röhm's orders rather than Hitler's. The necessity of organising a more dedicated élite personal guard was not lost on Hitler. This unit had to consist of men of proven calibre, of 'Nordic' blood and of good character, and have an unequivocal allegiance to Hitler. Its role would be both bodyguard and spearhead, to protect both Hitler and important members of his party.

At this time Hitler and his 'party comrades' were relentlessly campaigning to increase the NSDAP's membership and were beginning to travel outside Bavaria, into areas where allegiance was local rather than to Hitler himself. In March 1923 his bodyguard consisted of just two men, Josef Berchtold and Julius Schreck, who called themselves the Stabswache, or Staff Guard. Two months later a new unit, the *Stosstrupp Adolf Hitler*, commanded by Josef Berchtold, was formed. In August 1923, a certain Heinrich Himmler joined the NSDAP, and four months later he found himself carrying the imperial war flag during the 9 November Munich Putsch, when Hitler attempted to take over Bavaria. The putsch ended in a fiasco: some Nazi Party members were killed and the rest surrendered their weapons, identified themselves to the police and returned home, while their leaders were arrested. Hitler was imprisoned and the NSDAP banned. Himmler returned to Landshut where he sold advertising space in the *Völkischer Beobachter*, a right-wing Munich newspaper. He acted as secretary to Gregor Strasser, who, in February 1925, agreed to disband his National Freedom Movement and assimilate it into the reformed NSDAP. Strasser was appointed Reich Propaganda Leader of the NSDAP in September 1926, and Himmler accompanied him to party headquarters as his secretary.

Hitler, looking back on the period immediately after his release from Landsberg in December 1924, described the early days of the SS thus: 'When I came out of Landsberg everything was broken up and scattered in sometimes rival bands. I told myself then that I needed a bodyguard, even a restricted one, but made up of men who would be enlisted without conditions, even to march against their own brothers, only 20 men to a city (on condition that one could count on them absolutely) rather than a dubious mass. It was Maurice, Schreck and Heiden who formed in Munich the first

ABOVE: Members of the *Stosstrupp* (Shock Troop) *Adolf Hitler*, whom Hitler described as 'the first group of toughs'. The man in the centre with a moustache is Julius Schreck, who set up the Shock Troop. Their uniform is very similar to that of the SA, the only major difference being the black ski caps.

group of "toughs" and were thus the origins of the SS; but it was with Himmler that the SS became an extraordinary body of men, devoted to an ideal, loyal unto death.'

EARLY SS ENTRY STANDARDS

In April 1925, Hitler ordered his chauffeur and personal bodyguard, Julius Schreck, to raise a new shock troop. A few weeks later it was named the Schutzstaffel – Protection Squad. The new SS was to be organised on a national basis, and in September 1925 Julius Schreck sent a circular letter to all regional groups of the NSDAP asking them to form an SS, the strength of which was fixed by the SA at one officer and 10 men. This was the beginning of the so-called Zehnerstaffel, or Groups of Ten. Membership was to be exclusive: applicants had to have two sponsors, be between 25 and 35, registered with the police as residents of five years' standing, and be strong and healthy. Those not to be admitted were gossip-mongers, habitual drunkards and other 'delinquents'. Schreck was replaced by Berchtold, who in turn was replaced in March 1927 by his deputy, Eduard Heiden.

The SA kept an eye on SS expansion, and local SA commanders often used the SS for the most demeaning tasks. The SS was not allowed to form units in towns where the SA was under strength, nor recruit more than 10 per cent of the strength of the SA. By 1928 the SS still had only 280 members. Himmler's organising ability had not gone unnoticed, though, and he was appointed Deputy SS Leader and then National Leader in January 1929, with the rank of SS-Oberführer. He commanded approximately 1000 men, but to the SA this colourless bureaucrat posed little threat; he was just the man to command the SS and assure its continued subordination to the SA. But the bureaucrat had other ideas.

LEFT: Massed flags of the SA during a Nazi Party rally in the 1920s. The brownshirt Sturmabteilung (SA) – Storm Troops – were originally formed by Ernst Röhm to protect Nazi speakers at public meetings. The uniforms and prospect of violence appealed to many ex-Freikorps members, and the SA's membership grew accordingly: 2000 in 1926, 60,000 in 1930 and nearly three million by the time Hitler came to power in 1933. However, it soon became clear that the SA contained many disparate elements.

BELOW: Hitler inspecting an SA guard. In uniform the leader of the Nazi Party was careful to wear few decorations. These included his Iron Cross and wound badge, both earned during World War I. The only National Socialist badges he wore were the Golden Party Badge and Blood Order. In this way he hoped the masses would identify with him and his party. This, combined with his undoubted oratorical skills, helped to increase the appeal of the Nazis in the 1920s.

BELOW: SA and Nazi Party members take a break during one of the many NSDAP marches during the late 1920s. At first the SS was under the control of the SA, and the latter made sure the SS did not pose a threat. The SS was restricted to a maximum of only 10 per cent of the SA strength in each area, and the SS could only raise units in an area when the SA force in that area was at full strength. The SA regarded the SS as being élitist, while the SS resented its treatment at the hands of the SA. It was a state of affairs which could not last indefinitely, but in the late 1920s it suited Hitler to play these opposing factions against each other to allow him to concentrate on gaining power.

RIGHT: Though the SA was responsible for keeping order at Nazi Party meetings, Hitler soon realised that it was not unquestionably loyal. He therefore decided to create a new force. As he himself wrote: 'I told myself then that I needed a bodyguard, even a very restricted one, but made up of men who would be enlisted unconditionally, ready even to march against their own brothers.' Thus did the SS come into existence in 1925, following Hitler's release from Landsberg in December 1924. The term Schutz Staffel was reportedly thought up by Hermann Göring, a reference to aircraft that flew on escort duties during his service with the famed Richthofen squadron in World War I.

LEFT: SS-Brigadeführer Julius Schreck. An early member of the SA, he went on to form the *Stosstrupp Adolf Hitler* and, in 1925, the Schutzkommando, which was charged with Hitler's safety. A close friend of the Führer, in 1936 he contracted cerebrospinal meningitis and died. Hitler gave his former chauffeur a state funeral.

BELOW: Heinrich Himmler, one-time chicken farmer and later Reichsführer-SS. He joined the NSDAP in 1923, and was appointed head of the SS in 1929. He gave so much time to the SS that his business failed and his marriage fell apart, but his efforts ensured that the SS became much more prominent in Nazi Germany.

LEFT: SS-Obergruppenführer Walter Buch. Born in 1883, he was the son of a prominent judge. He served in World War I, rising to the rank of major, and after the war was a member of several Freikorps. He then joined the SA and took part in the abortive Munich Beer Hall Putsch. Subsequently he became a member of the SS. He was typical of the people Hitler surrounded himself with in the 1920s: tough, nationalist and ruthless. He was also violently anti-Semitic, writing in an article: 'The Jew is not a human being. He is an appearance of putrescence.' He committed suicide in prison after the war.

LEFT: The Coburg Badge, an award instituted on 14 October 1932 in recognition of the tenth anniversary of the Nazi victory over the communists in Coburg. This action was to enter Nazi folklore. To answer in the affirmative to the question, 'Where you at Coburg?', was a sign of being an ardent Nazi. The badge was declared an official party and national decoration in a decree signed by Hitler on 6 November 1936. It had been the highest party award since its inception in 1932, and was held in greater esteem than the Blood Order itself. It was a rare award; indeed, only 436 names entered on the official party roll of recipients were entitled to wear it.

RIGHT: The figure on the left is wearing an early Allgemeine-SS uniform. The kepi on his head is adorned with the first-pattern SS eagle, which had a chinless skull. The death's head badge would later become the symbol of the Waffen-SS.

LEFT: Ernst Röhm (left), leader of the SA, standing next to an Allgemeine-SS officer in early uniform. Röhm was a bully and adventurer, who one day dreamed that his SA would replace the German Army as a true national defence force. This and other ideas, which differed wildly from Hitler's, would lead to his execution when the Nazis came to power. On the right is Willy Liebel, who represented Nazi interests in Nuremberg so well that when they came to power he was made mayor on 15 March 1933.

ABOVE: A mounted SS-Totenkopfverbände NCO at Dachau concentration camp (on the horse's hindquarters can be seen the brand of the German Federation for Breeding and Testing of Thoroughbreds). Dachau is a village a short distance from Munich. It once had the reputation as the home of a Bavarian artistic community, but during the Nazi era had more sinister connotations. To the German public in the early Nazi period Dachau was portrayed as a school for good citizenship, and at the November 1933 elections 2154 of the 2242 inmates were declared to have voted Nazi (unsurprisingly!). Later thousands were to be murdered at the camp.

LEFT: A picture that conveys the power of Himmler's Allgemeine-SS officer corps: (from left to right) Theodor Eicke, Karl Wolff and Josef 'Sepp' Dietrich (who is wearing the lion-headed sabre of the German Army). Wolff was Himmler's personal adjutant, and was later to be the liaison officer between Himmler and Hitler. He shared Himmler's views on how the SS should be developed, and also believed in Teutonic mysticism. He was dismissed in 1943 because he insisted on divorcing his wife, against Himmler's wishes (Himmler could sanction the death of millions, but he applied a strict moral code when it came to his subordinates).

RIGHT: A member of the SS-Totenkopfverbände during his training at Dachau concentration camp (note his blank collar patches). The men who became camp guards during the 1930s laid the basis for the creation of the *Totenkopf* Division. Their commander, Theodor Eicke, established two camp policies that would have a significant effect on the history of the Third Reich. First was the conduct of the SS guards, who were taught to treat prisoners with fanatical hatred as they were enemies of the state. Second, he laid down regulations for use against camp prisoners, which would endure until the Third Reich fell, and which codified mass murder.

BELOW: The 120-strong Stabswache (Headquarters Guard) formed up on the steps of the Feldherrnhalle, the Nazi Party's headquarters, in Munich in 1930. 'Sepp' Dietrich is second from the left in the front row. The Stabswache moved into the former Imperial Cadet barracks on the outskirts of Berlin after the Nazis came to power. In September 1933 it was officially renamed *Leibstandarte SS Adolf Hitler* (*SS Bodyguard Regiment Adolf Hitler*). During the war Hitler's bodyguard became one of the Third Reich's premier fighting formations, becoming an élite panzer division. Dietrich was described by Hitler as being 'cunning and brutal'.

ABOVE: SS-Totenkopfverbände men relax at the end of a hard day's training near Munich in 1933. Eicke undoubtedly produced brutal guards and later Waffen-SS soldiers, who were imbued with unsurpassed camaraderie and toughness.

LEFT: This picture, taken at Dachau, shows SS-Totenkopfverbände men in their SS drill clothing and displaying blank collar patches. The drill clothing was worn to preserve and protect the black uniform, and was produced in various patterns and colours, which could vary from light grey to off-white.

BELOW: Members of the SS-Totenkopfverbände relax at the end of a day's training. By the end of the 1920s Himmler had begun the process of separating the SS from the SA. Racial criteria were brought into recruitment to sift the large number of applications from ex-Freikorps and unemployed bourgeois volunteers. To distinguish the SS from the SA, SS men began to wear black caps and ties, and black edging on their swastika arm-bands. For its part the army, which perceived Röhm and his SA as rivals, took a favourable view to the SS. This, plus Himmler's organisational skills, resulted in the SS's growth, albeit at a steady rate, giving him a personal power base.

LEFT: A member of the SS-Totenkopfverbände at work as an orderly. The board behind him is a duty roster, giving details of the Diensteinteilung Für Die SS Largerwache, and lists a Pohl as watch commander. Concentration camp duty was an integral part of SS-Totenkopfverbände training. Members spent three weeks in every month training, followed by one week of concentration camp guard duty. The three-week training programme concentrated on political training, and was split into three areas: the history of the Nazi Party, the history and racial beliefs of the SS, and an analysis of the enemies of National Socialism (the Jews, freemasonry, bolshevism and the churches).

CHAPTER TWO

Himmler's Troops

Expansion and development of the SS

In 1930 the political situation in Germany degenerated into near civil war. The socialists and the Communist Party fielded armed militia, to which the SA and SS replied with force. Some 10 SS men were killed and hundreds wounded during the violent street battles with the Rötfrontkämpferbund, or Red Front Fighters' Association. This civil unrest suited the NSDAP, especially with the 1933 elections approaching, and it was able to create the illusion that it held the key to Germany's problems.

The plan worked, for three years later, on 30 January 1933, Hitler became Chancellor. The SS, which had 2727 men in 1930, had secretly recruited 52,000 more members by this date. On 1 April 1933, Himmler became Commander of the Bavarian Political Police as well as Polizeipräsident of Munich. This enabled him to gradually gain control of the police network, except in Prussia where Hermann Göring was Minister of the Interior.

TOWARDS THE TOTALITARIAN STATE

Related to Göring was SS-Oberführer Rudolf Diels, who joined the Prussian Ministry of the Interior in 1930, becoming a high-ranking police official. He was a Nazi Party member by 1932, and subsequently married Göring's cousin. He persuaded Göring that a secret police force was necessary to monitor the activities of the communists, a view reinforced by the Reichstag fire on 27 February 1933. The work of a demented pyromaniac, it resulted in the Decree for the Protection of People and State. This gave police powers to

LEFT: A youthful SS-Rottenführer displays an edelweiss collar patch. SS-Fuss-Standarte (SS Foot Regiment) 87 utilised the edelweiss insignia on the right collar instead of the number system. Note the Nazi Party badge on his tie.

OPPOSITE: Members of the SS-Totenkopfverbände.

the SA and SS: 25,000 SA and 15,000 SS men were issued with firearms and deployed as auxiliary policemen. This also empowered the police presidents to take anyone into protective custody considered to be a political opponent in the broadest sense of the term. The fire also provided Hitler with an excuse to put the Nazi Party's left-wing members into prisons and makeshift unofficial camps, or 'wild man camps', so called due to their lack of supervision and the frightful stories of brutality which came from them.

THE INSIDIOUS TENTACLES OF POWER

A decree of 26 April 1933 established the Geheime Staatspolizei (Gestapa), later renamed Geheime Staatspolizei (Gestapo), the infamous Nazi Secret State Police, to be headed by Diels. The Gestapo became the target for Himmler, bringing him into conflict with Diels. The latter lost and fled the country in the autumn of 1933, allowing Himmler to usurp the organisation.

By this time the SS was divided into two distinct groups: the Allgemeine-SS, which fulfilled a police function and was basically part time, and the newly created Bewaffnete-SS, or

Armed SS which was military in appearance and full time. Himmler had himself to be ruthlessly ambitious, and he gathered around him like-minded individuals.

THE SS-TOTENKOPFVERBÄNDE

Himmler's man of steel was Theodor Eicke, who was to play a key role in the liquidation of the SA Chief of Staff, Ernst Röhm, and his supporters during the so-called Night of the Long Knives at the end of June 1934, when Hitler purged the SA. A decree of 26 July 1934 recognised the part the SS had played in the action and promoted it to the status of an independent organisation within the NSDAP. That summer most of the 'wild man camps' were closed. The remaining SA camps were removed from the jurisdiction of the civil authorities and taken over by the SS. The first full-time SS concentration camp unit was recruited from members of the Allgemeine-SS and placed under the overall command of the SS District South, which made it a depository for its unwanted personnel. Conditions inside the camp were poor, and in June 1934 Eicke took command. He improved conditions, lifted the morale and discipline of his men and formulated service regulations for both guards and prisoners, which remained virtually unchanged until the end of the war. In recognition Himmler appointed him Inspector of Concentration Camps and head of the SS-Totenkopfverbände (Death's Head Formations), the concentration camp guards, in 1934. The inspectorate was established at Oranienburg, near Berlin, and the SS-Totenkopfverbände was enlarged and reorganised into five numbered sturmbanne, or battalions: I *Oberbayern*, II *Elbe*, III *Sachsen*, IV *Ostfriesland* and V *Thüringen*.

The SS now entered a period of consolidation, in which it developed its command structure, armed units, concentration camps and security service. Himmler set about implementing his theories of a racially and ideologically élite force, and creating a future German 'master race' through the SS-controlled Lebensborn network of maternity homes. The SS now entered its second phase of rapid expansion.

Within three hours of Hindenburg's death on 2 August 1934, Göbbels, Nazi Propaganda Minister, announced the fusing of the two roles of Chancellor and President. The only barrier between Hitler and unrestrained power had fallen; he was now in the position to dictate and reward. In return for the services the SS had rendered in the Night of the Long Knives, it was allowed to form militarised formations. The chiefs of the three branches of the Wehrmacht were officially advised on 24 September 1934 of the creation of these militarised units, called SS-Verfügungstruppe.

THE *LEIBSTANDARTE* IS BORN

Hitler decided that he also needed a Praetorian Guard, as the protection rendered by the Reichswehr and police elements could not in his eyes be entirely relied upon. Without delay he therefore decreed that a new full-time armed SS unit be formed, the main role of which would be to escort him wherever he was in Germany. Josef 'Sepp' Dietrich, one of Hitler's closest associates, was entrusted with the formation of the unit.

Dietrich undertook the task with zeal, and by 17 March 1933 the embryo of a new Headquarters Guard named the SS Stabswache *Berlin* was founded. It comprised 120 hand-picked volunteers, some of whom were former members of the *Stosstrupp Adolf Hitler*. Two months later the unit was reformed as the SS Sonderkommando *Zossen* and enlarged with three training companies. The terms of engagement for the unit were expanded, and it could now be employed for armed police and anti-terrorist activities, as well for guard duties. There was another metamorphosis during the next months when a further three companies were formed as the SS Sonderkommando *Jüterbog*.

A rally was held on 31 August 1933 to marked the Nazi accession to power. Known as the Parteitag des Siegers, or Victor's Party Rally, it was a fitting occasion for Hitler to formally recognise the *Adolf Hitler* SS-Standarte, and the dedication of the SS-Standarten (SS regiments) took place. They were formed from SS-Sonderkommando *Zossen* and SS-Sonderkommando *Jüterbog*. SS-Grüppenführer 'Sepp' Dietrich received the banner with the name 'Adolf Hitler' on the box that surmounted it. The two sonderkommandos were granted the honour and right to wear the name 'Adolf Hitler' on a cuff band on the left arm. The merged formation was renamed the *Leibstandarte SS Adolf Hitler*.

REWARD FOR SERVICES RENDERED

The *Leibstandarte* was used in the Röhm Putsch, during which it arrested suspects and carried out executions. The number of executions undertaken by it firing squads is unknown, but it is reported that there were in the order of 40 executioners employed. The *Leibstandarte*'s 'first blooding' was over when the shooting finally ended on 2 July 1934. For their loyalty and involvement, Hitler promised it would be made a fully equipped regiment. The *Leibstandarte* was further honoured in early October 1934 when it was decided that it should be fully motorised. At this time the Reichswehr in the main was still horse-drawn, and this deci-

sion led to hushed whispers of discontent in military circles. By 14 December 1934, the *Leibstandarte* consisted of one Staff, three motorised infantry battalions, one motorcycle company, one motor company, one signals platoon, one armoured car platoon and one regimental band.

On 16 March 1935 Hitler announced to the German parliament, in direct contravention of the Treaty of Versailles, that he had reintroduced military conscription and officially established the SS-Verfügungstruppe. The full-time SS now consisted of three distinct branches, each having its own command structure: the SS-Verfügungstruppe, the SS-Totenkopfverbände and the Security Service. The Allgemeine-SS encompassed the remainder, which by the outbreak of World War II numbered some 240,000 part-time members. These were kept in readiness by a small regular staff in case of internal strife. In reality Allgemeine-SS personnel were called up for service in both the armed forces and Waffen-SS, to such an extent that many Allgemeine-SS units survived in name only.

THE ROLE OF THE SS-VERFÜGUNGSTRUPPE

On 17 August 1938, Hitler stated that the SS-Verfügungstruppe was an armed force at his personal disposal, not a part of the armed or police forces. Therefore it could be trained by the Reichsführer-SS in Nazi theories of race, and manned by volunteers who had completed their commitment in the Reichsarbeitsdienst, the Reich Labour Service. The Führer's decree also indicated that in wartime elements of the SS-Totenkopfverbände would reinforce the SS-Verfügungstruppe. Mobilised SS units would operate under army jurisdiction, but still owe their allegiance to the Nazi Party. Also, in the event of an emergency within Germany the SS-Verfügungstruppe would be under Hitler's control. The army regarded the creation of armed SS units as a betrayal of its role as sole arms bearer of the state, but could do little to stop the rise of Himmler's élite.

LEFT: Armed SS on the streets of Innsbruck on 4 April 1938 during the *Anschluss*, when Hitler occupied Austria. The *Leibstandarte* and the *Deutschland* and *Germania* Regiments took part in the invasion. Soon after the annexation, the SS *Der Führer* Regiment was raised in Vienna.

LEFT: The Golden Party Badge. Hitler decreed that all members of the NSDAP who had a membership number below 100,000 and an unbroken record of service should receive a special version of the Party Badge. The award is variously referred to as the Golden Party Badge, Golden Party Decoration or the NSDAP Decoration. Where the badge denotes veteran membership, the member's number is stamped on the reverse, whereas if it is a decoration the reverse has 'A.H.' for Adolf Hitler and the date of the award inscribed upon it. Many SS members were awarded this coveted badge.

LEFT: Victor Lutze, commander of the SA after Röhm's execution, gives an address at the 1935 Nazi Party Rally. In the background is the Blood Banner, which was carried during the Munich Beer Hall Putsch and was used by Hitler to dedicate new flags. Lutze was killed in 1943.

ABOVE: The Blood Order. Originally awarded to those who took part in the Munich Beer Hall Putsch, from May 1938 it was also given to party members who had performed outstanding service. Some 436 posthumous awards were made, the last being to Reinhard Heydrichs on 4 June 1942.

BELOW: Massed ranks of the SA stand in silence in salute in front of the Feldherrnhalle in Munich during a parade to commemorate the Beer Hall Putsch. Such parades were described as 'a uniquely holy event, in which the venerated cadre of the survivors silently re-enacted their march through the crowd-lined streets of the Bavarian capital in a bombastic travesty of the Passion Play'. The finale was a torch-lit, oath-taking ceremony for members of the SS-Verfügungstruppe, which took place before the Feldherrnhalle and the 16 smoking obelisks, each of which bore the name of the first fallen party faithful. These oaths were integral to the Nazi mystique.

LEFT: The Feldherrnhalle in Munich guarded by the SS-Totenkopfverbände. The eagle and swastika surmount a large bronze monument bearing the names of 16 National Socialists killed in front of the stone edifice during the abortive Beer Hall Putsch of 9 November 1923. This bronze monument was erected on the side of the Feldherrnhalle and was guarded by SA and SS troops. It was compulsory for passers-by to salute it. The bronze salute to those killed during the putsch was destroyed after the war in accordance with a directive of 13 May 1946 issued by the Allied Control Council for Germany. The Feldherrnhalle was not touched.

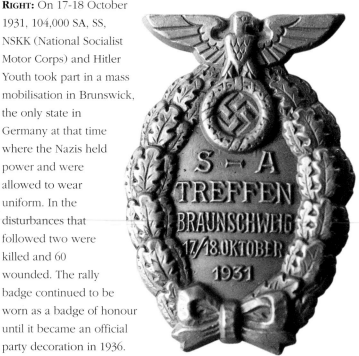

LEFT: The first Nazi Party Day was held in January 1923 and was a small affair, as were the two subsequent ones at Weimar in July 1926 and Nuremberg in August 1927. The fourth Party Day on 1-2 August 1929, though, was much larger, with 60,000 taking part, and was the last Party Day until the Nazis came to power in 1933. Every Party Day had its commemorative badge, which was worn only for the duration of the rally. The badge for Nuremberg in 1929, however, continued to be worn as a badge of honour.

RIGHT: On 17-18 October 1931, 104,000 SA, SS, NSKK (National Socialist Motor Corps) and Hitler Youth took part in a mass mobilisation in Brunswick, the only state in Germany at that time where the Nazis held power and were allowed to wear uniform. In the disturbances that followed two were killed and 60 wounded. The rally badge continued to be worn as a badge of honour until it became an official party decoration in 1936.

ABOVE: Members of Eicke's SS-Totenkopfverbände in their distinctive black uniforms pose for a group photograph. Eicke placed special emphasis on the development of camaraderie and esprit de corps among his men. In particular he believed that a good *esprit de corps* was the one intangible asset that made a unit totally invincible.

RIGHT: SA men marching in a torch-lit procession. Torches and floodlights became an established part of Nazi rallies; in one of them, 100 searchlights were mounted to direct their beams vertically in great columns of light. It prompted the British Ambassador to describe the scene as a 'cathedral of ice'.

LEFT: Members of the SS Security Guard, who were responsible for Hitler's personal safety, stand below the window of his new Chancellery as he appears to acknowledge the cheers of the crowd on his return to Berlin in July 1934. The mood of the SS guards appears to be relaxed.

ABOVE: The Nuremberg Party Day Badge of 1933. The Victors' Party Rally was held on 3 September 1933. SS-Gruppenführer 'Sepp' Dietrich, close friend of Hitler, assumed command of the *Adolf Hitler* Regiment, the forerunner of what was eventually to become the *Leibstandarte* Division.

THE *LEIBSTANDARTE*

Hitler's bodyguard was an élite within an élite. Each member took a personal oath of loyalty to Hitler, and even Himmler complained it was 'a law unto itself'.

BELOW: The *Leibstandarte* on parade. During the pre-war period the unit started to lag behind the rest of the SS-Verfügungstruppe with regard to military training. Indeed, Felix Steiner himself commented: 'It's pathetic. If the Führer realised what his blond gods can't do he would get rid of the lot of them.' The rest of the SS-Verfügungstruppe began to contemptuously refer to the *Leibstandarte* as the 'Asphalt Soldiers', due to their propensity to march on the parade ground.

RIGHT: Members of the *Leibstandarte* in their black parade uniforms in February 1938. This unit had a unique status within the armed SS, as stated by the historian Hans Buchheim: 'The Reich Chancellor had formed a body of armed men who had no place in the state or the party organisations, but was at the sole disposal of the Führer and pledged to him personally. Hitler had to render account to no-one for the use to which these men were put.' In this way it was a true Praetorian Guard.

BELOW: Officers of the *Leibstandarte* at Tempelhof airport in August 1933. They are, from left to right, Johansen, 'Sepp' Dietrich, Walter Stein and Max Hense.

Dietrich and his fellow officers realised that the *Leibstandarte* was not being taken seriously by the rest of the armed SS, and they set about rectifying this.

BELOW: Albert Stenwedel in front of the 11th Company, SS-Sonderkommando *Zossen*, Berlin 1933. The men are wearing the first-pattern field cap, which was identical to that of the Imperial Army.

RIGHT: The *Leibstandarte* drilling in 1935. Second from the left in the front row is Fritz Klingenberg, who won the Knight's Cross in April 1941 when he and a handful of men captured Belgrade.

ABOVE: Hitler on the podium at the 1933 Nuremberg Rally, which celebrated the Nazis' accession to power in January of that year. Each rally at Nuremberg was grander than the previous one and was designed to whip up emotions of frenzied support for Hitler and the Nazi Party. From 1934 Albert Speer began the design of a great auditorium at Nuremberg, in which future rallies would be held. Work continued on this project throughout World War II.

LEFT: German troops on parade in 1935 to salute the fallen of World War I. Hitler's Third Reich was a militaristic state, in which the military and political spheres were unified, as was the case in the armed SS. As one SS author later wrote: 'In the past, politics and the armed forces have often pursued divergent paths. The Waffen-SS provides the first example of the indissoluble unity of the two, in that concept and sword are welded into one, and the political determination brings such strength to the soldier's sword that it renders it invincible.'

RIGHT: Hitler at the 1934 Nuremberg Rally consecrates new standards by holding the Blood Banner (the flag carried during the 1923 Munich Putsch) in one hand and touching the new standard in the other. In this way the 'heroic essence' of the Blood Banner would flow through the Führer to the new flag. Note how Hitler is holding the banner as he shakes hands with the SA man. Jakob Grimminger is carrying the Blood Banner.

BELOW: Massed ranks at the Reich Party Day of 1934. In that year Hitler remarked to Himmler: 'In our Reich of the future, the SS and police will possess the necessary authority in their relations with other citizens only if they have a soldierly charac-ter ... For this reason it will be necessary for our SS and police to prove themselves at the front.' The armed SS was established a year later.

LEFT: Reichsführer-SS and Chief of the German Police Heinrich Himmler photographed with the leaders of the SS. At first Himmler envisaged the armed SS as nothing more than a formation for maintaining internal order within Germany in time of war, thus leaving the army free to fight external enemies. That said, both Hitler and Himmler believed that the SS-Verfügungstruppe would have to be blooded to lend it credibility for the 'hard tasks' it would have to perform in the future.

BELOW: Allgemeine-SS officers hold back an enthusiastic crowd at the Reich Party Day in September 1935. By this time the ranks of both the SA and SS had swelled considerably. After the Nazis had gained power in 1933, for example, the SS increased in size to 50,000, while the SA, 500,000 strong at the beginning of 1933, grew to nearly three million men by the year's end. These newcomers were disparagingly entitled 'March Violets' by those who had been in the party since the early 1920s. Nevertheless, Himmler was anxious to attract as many 'racially qualified' recruits to his SS as possible.

ABOVE: Reichsführer-SS Heinrich Himmler officially presents a new standard to the *Leibstandarte* on behalf of Hitler at Metz. This is the second version of the banner, and was based on the design for the Führerstandarte designed by Carl Diebitsch, who was also responsible for this standard. The standard was produced by the firm Fahnen Hoffmann of Berlin. Though technically under Himmler's control, the *Leibstandarte* was in reality a law unto itself, and its commander, Dietrich, took no notice of Himmler's orders. The gates of its Lichterfelde barracks were closed to even the Reichsführer-SS.

LEFT: SS-Gruppenführer Dietrich presents a report to SA-Obergruppenführer Wilhelm Bruckner, Hitler's chief personal adjutant. Bruckner commanded the SA Munich Regiment during the Munich Putsch, and was one of Hitler's co-defendants in the subsequent trial. He left the NSDAP in May 1925 after disagreeing with Hitler, but rejoined five years later. On 20 February 1934, he was appointed to the post of chief personal adjutant to Hitler. Through Bruckner Dietrich ran the *Leibstandarte* very much as he wished.

Östr. Legion Lechfeld 1933

ABOVE: The Austrian Legion drawn up for inspection at Lechfeld in 1933. It was composed of Austrian Nazis under the control of Himmler (the Austrian SS never fell under the jurisdiction of the Austrian Nazi Party or the Austrian SA). On 25 July 1934, a group of Austrian SS men murdered the Austrian Chancellor, Engelbert Dollfuss, in an attempt to bring about union with Nazi Germany. However, the attempt failed and Hitler, despite having provoked the action (he allowed active Austrian Nazis to find refuge in the SS camp at Lechfeld, just across the Austrian border), was forced to issue a denunciation, especially when Mussolini moved four divisions to the Brenner Pass to indicate he would not tolerate a Austro-German union.

BELOW: The cuff bands of the *Der Führer* and *Deutschland* Regiments. The latter was originally named the 2nd SS Regiment, but assumed the title 1st SS Regiment when the *Leibstandarte* dropped out of the regimental numbering sequence in 1934. The *Der Führer* Regiment was originally titled the 3rd SS Regiment. Following the union with Austria in 1938, Hitler ordered SS-Oberführer Georg Keppler to start organising the unit. Unlike the *Leibstandarte*, *Germania* and *Deutschland* Regiments, its cadre was men transferred from other units of the SS-Verfügungstruppe and not from the Allgemeine-SS. Later it would become part of the *Das Reich* Division, fighting with distinction throughout World War II.

BELOW: SS-Totenkopfverbände members, in parade uniform and sporting the 1916-model steel helmet, stand guard at Dachau. The coming to power of the Nazis had necessitated a reorganisation of the concentration camp guard units, both as a result of Theodor Eicke wishing to tighten up control and the large numbers of prisoners the camps had to accommodate. By April 1938, therefore, the organisation of the SS-Totenkopfverbände was fixed at four regiments, each of three battalions, which in turn were made up of three companies.

ABOVE: SS-Sturmbannführer Carl-Heinz Frühauf, typical of many who joined the SS-Verfügungstruppe in the early 1930s and who later helped forge the military reputation of the Waffen-SS. Between April 1934 and March 1935 he was an instructor at the SS Sports School at Sternberg/Mecklenberg, and on 9 November 1937 was promoted to SS-Oberscharführer. From November 1937 to June 1938 he held various posts in the 1st and 3rd Companies of the *Germania* Regiment. In March 1944 he was fighting in northern Russia with the Waffen-SS, at the Battle of Narva. He led a counterattack which threw back a Russian assault after hand-to-hand fighting, for which he was awarded the Knight's Cross.

ABOVE: A group of SS-Verfügungstruppe soldiers take a break during a training exercise. The two men on the right are each wearing two cuff bands. The man smoking sports the cuff band of the *Germania* Regiment, while the other carries that of the *Leibstandarte*. The upper bands are indistinguishable. The Germany Army, jealous of its position as sole arms bearer of the state, regarded the creation of armed units within the SS as a threat. In its eyes it was but a short step to the creation of an independent SS army beyond its control. In the event, though, SS units remained mostly under army control during the war.

LEFT: A youthful Carl-Heinz Frühauf in SS uniform. Heavy National Socialist indoctrination, combined with the military training as laid down by Felix Steiner and Paul Hausser, had created a new type of soldier in Germany in the 1930s, imbued with tough ruthlessness, recklessness and total dedication. Men like Frühauf were summed up by Himmler when he later stated during the war: 'Their lives are of value to them only as long as they can be used to serve the Führer. They toss them away for all the world as if they were hand grenades when the need, or even the opportunity arises.'

ABOVE: Philipp Bouhler (left), who rose to the rank of SS-Obergruppenführer, talking with the oldest SA man at the time (holder of the Blood Order) in the centre and SA commander Victor Lutze on the right. Bouhler was a distinctly nasty character. Having been badly wounded in World War I, he followed a career in publishing after hostilities ceased and became an early member of the Nazi Party. In 1939, together with Dr Karl Brandt, he was in charge of the euthanasia programme which was charged with getting rid of the mentally ill, though such was the public outrage that Hitler was forced to abandon it. At the end of the war both Bouhler and his wife committed suicide rather than fall into Allied hands.

RIGHT: Carl-Heinz Frühauf stands beside one of the SS-Verfügungstruppe's vehicles just prior to the outbreak of World War II. At this time relations between the SS and the army were at a low ebb. There were frequent fights between members of the army and armed SS. An SS report at this time commented on the 'social reserve of the army officers, and the open aggression of their men, which sours all our efforts to the contrary'. This hostility continued during the war, though to a lesser degree.

CHAPTER THREE

Forging an Élite

SS indoctrination and training

It had always been the desire of Eicke, Steiner and Hausser that the SS-Verfügungstruppe would benefit from the highest standards of training available. To this end a special Inspectorate of the SS-Verfügungstruppe was established to supervise administration and military training, and weld the far-flung and mainly ill-trained

LEFT: Members of the Deutsche Jungvolk (German Young People's Organisation) watch spellbound at a Nazi Party rally.

OPPOSITE: SS volunteers swearing their allegiance over an SS Honour Sword, an almost mystical occasion which bound the individual to Adolf Hitler for life.

units of the SS-Verfügungstruppe into an efficient fighting force. But why did so many young Germans volunteer, and what guidelines were laid down for their membership of the SS generally, and SS-Totenkopfverbände and SS-Verfügung-struppe especially?

SS-VERFÜGUNGSTRUPPE RECRUITMENT

University trained products of the National Youth Movement were encouraged to join the SS. These young men, predominately lawyers and economists, gravitated to the Sicherheitsdienst (Heydrich's Security Service). The fledgling SS-Verfügungstruppe's officer cadres also attracted some of these volunteers, though a greater proportion were middle-class soldiers who transferred from the small standing army. To attract members of the officer class, discreet political overtures were made to certain highly respected members of the old German aristocracy. Surprisingly, several of its prominent members responded favourably, including the Grand Duke of Mecklenburg and the Princes of Waldeck and Hess. Cleansing programmes were also implemented, with the result that between 1933 and 1935 some 60,000 men were expelled from the SS. They were expelled if they were of 'Jewish blood', or were criminals, homosexuals, alcoholics or members of the 'professionally unemployed'. Strict prerequisites for acceptance were introduced: racial purity, physical fitness, height and the lack of a criminal record. The

result of these polices was that, by 1938, 12 per cent of SS officers holding the rank of SS-Standartenführer or higher came from the aristocracy.

THE CONCEPT OF BLOOD AND SOIL

At the other end of the scale, farmers' sons were another group whose recruitment into the SS was actively encouraged by Himmler, with his quaint rustic idealism. These ideals were encapsulated in a book written by SS-Obergruppen-führer Walter Darré, who propounded that the Germans were both farmers and warriors. There was no clear division between peasantry and nobility, since every free man was noble, as he could bear arms. He believed Nordism in Germany to be on the wane due to a decline among the peasantry. It was therefore fundamental to create a new nobility, composed not of individuals but of families. The concept of blood and earth was thus intimately linked. But Christianity was considered an evil influence, destroying the original concept of Germanism.

Himmler embodied these thoughts into SS ideology, though his anti-Christian policies deterred many men who would have volunteered and would have been found suitable. But under these conditions, and the rigorous standards now employed, the supply of acceptable recruits began to dwindle dramatically. Before the war, though, this was not a cause for alarm, and only added to the SS's exclusivity.

LEFT: An SS propaganda postcard, a simple yet effective way of reinforcing the view that the SS was a special organisation. Its theme is strongly Nordic, as propounded by the Nazis: the fighter on the left contrasts with the mother and child overseen by the grandfather on the right.

ed on educational qualifications, and before 1938 40 per cent of SS recruits had only received what could be termed primary school education. Insistence on being able to prove Aryan descent, being in good physical and mental condition and to have clean police records were viewed as being more important.

At the age of 18 a Hitlerjugend (Hitler Youth) became an SS-Bewerber (applicant). On the Reich's Party Day of the same year, he was accepted as an SS-Anwärter (candidate) and given an SS identity card. After a short probationary period he took the oath of allegiance to Adolf Hitler. At the age of 19 or 19 and a half, depending on when his age group was called, he went into the Labour Service and then into the armed forces

MEMBERSHIP OF THE SS

He returned to the SS, still as a candidate, if he elected not to remain in the armed forces as a regular or noncommissioned officer candidate after his two years' service. The candidate was given special philosophical training, the principles of the SS being thoroughly explained, in particular the marriage order and code of honour. Subject to fulfilling all the special requirements, the SS candidate was finally accepted as an SS man. On 9 November, after his return from the armed forces, at a special ceremony, he vowed that he and his relations would forever observe the basic laws of the SS. The newly ordained SS man was given the right to wear the SS dagger, and from that day forth it was his right and duty to defend his honour, according to the code of honour of the Black Corps. He remained in the Allgemeine-SS on the active list until he was 35 years of age, when, upon application, he was placed on the SS reserve list.

What of the SS-Totenkopfverbände?. To join the *Leibstandarte* or SS-Verfügungstruppe, a recruit had to be at least 5ft 11in and later 6ft 0.5in tall and between the ages of 17 and 22. For the SS-Totenkopfverbände the height restriction was only 5ft 7.5in, which was later reduced to 5ft 6.7in tall, with an upper age limit of 26. Neither organisation insist-

THE POLICIES OF THEODOR EICKE

Theodor Eicke stamped his own rigid views on the SS-Totenkopfverbände. He believed that it was an élite within the élite. This concept grew from the fact that the most dangerous political enemies of the state were incarcerated in the concentration camps, and Hitler had given sole responsibility for guarding and running the camps to the SS-Totenkopfverbände. Eicke pressed home his principles relentlessly in orders, circulars and memoranda. The whole of the SS-Totenkopfverbände training he based on élitism, toughness and comradeship, together with a regime of ruthless discipline. The slightest infraction of the rules brought harsh and often brutal punishment.

Each month was split into three weeks of training, followed by one week of guard duty within the concentration camp. The training, both political and military, was designed to instil a state of mind, shape the attitude, and colour the outlook of the SS-Totenkopfverbände man. Participation in camp guard duty exposed him to the prisoners and conditions in the camps, an experience Eicke felt would underpin the lessons learned during training, strengthening the resolve that the prisoners were inferior but implacable enemies of the German state. The SS-Totenkopfverbände's behaviour towards the prisoners created an atmosphere conducive to political fanaticism, which gave rise to the excesses later committed by the *Totenkopf* Division during the war.

What of SS military training? Felix Steiner held revolutionary ideas compared to traditional training, which placed an emphasis on drill. He believed strongly in the creation of élite, highly mobile groups whose training put the emphasis on individual responsibility and military teamwork rather than mindless obedience. His ideas had been formulated and refined during World War I, when he served as commander of a machine-gun company, witnessing the formation of 'battle groups', which had greatly impressed him. They were made up from selected men, withdrawn from the trenches and formed into ad hoc assault groups.

STEINER'S TRAINING ROUTINES

As their value became recognised, Steiner's reforms gradually filtered throughout the SS-Verfügungstruppe. In concert with his 'battle group' ideology he promoted a strict physical programme, together with a regime of cleanliness. One recruit in three failed basic training the first time round. However, for successful candidates there was the reward of the passing-out parade, where the SS oath was taken. It was taken at 2200 hours on the occasion of the 9 November anniversary celebrations. These have been described as a 'uniquely holy event, in which the venerated cadre of the survivors of the Munich Putsch silently re-enacted their march through the crowd-lined streets of the Bavarian capital in a bombastic travesty of the Passion Play'. The finale was the torch-lit oath-taking ceremony for candidates of the SS-Verfügungstruppe, which took place in Hitler's presence before the Feldherrnhalle and the 16 smoking obelisks, each of which bore the name of the first fallen party faithful. The oath was a major ingredient in the SS mystique, binding each successful candidate in unswerving loyalty to Adolf Hitler.

The candidate now had to spend a year in one of the SS infantry or cavalry schools, before returning to Munich to swear another oath binding himself to obey Himmler's marriage laws. This was an attempt to replace the Christian rites of marriage, christening and death. Marriages no longer took place in churches but in the open under a lime tree, or in an SS building decorated with life runes, fir twigs and sunflowers. The proof of Aryan ancestry was designed to protect racial and physical purity. The recruit became a fully fledged SS man, and officers of SS-Untersturmführer rank and above were given the SS dagger.

To be eligible for a commission in the SS-Verfügungstruppe, officer cadets had to have served for a minimum of two years in the ranks, which initially meant in the Reichswehr. Officers enlisted for 25 years, NCOs for 12 and privates for four, with basic training being the same for all groups. Officers had to undertake an intensive combat course, which included tests of courage such as having to dig a foxhole in front of an advancing tank. More significant were live-firing exercises with machine guns, mortars and artillery, which were designed to introduce men to genuine battlefield conditions.

SS SOLDIERS — A NEW BREED OF WARRIORS

An innovation introduced by Eicke and emulated by Steiner was designed to break down the rigid divisions between ranks, which existed in the army. Officers and NCOs were encouraged to talk and mix with their men to get to know them as individuals. They competed in teams against each other on the sports field. Off duty they addressed each other as kamerad, rather than by rank.

The consequences of SS training was to dehumanise the troops. They placed little value on their own lives, and even less on those of their enemies. It was thus but a short step to shoot prisoners and commit atrocities against civilians. The seeds of courage of the highest order, and crimes of the most appalling nature, had thus been sowed.

LEFT: A Nazi pageant in Munich in 1938 to commemorate the opening of a cultural centre built there, which was designed to show off German culture and art. The SS was integral to the celebrations, its members being dressed up as Teutonic Knights, who were heroes to the Nazi Party.

RIGHT: Young German girls, members of the Bund deutscher Mädel (B.d.M.), League of German Girls. This organisation was founded in 1930 as the female equivalent of the Hitler Youth. After Hitler came to power, service in the B.d.M. was mandatory for all girls between the ages of 14 and 21. Women were expected to bear lots of children for the Third Reich in order to create a 'pure' Aryan race of Germans who would colonise the conquered areas of eastern Europe. The urgent need for new blood prompted Himmler to consider forcing couples to divorce if, after five years of marriage, they were still childless.

LEFT: Two young girls of the Bund deutscher Mädel with a young boy undergoing Nazi training (note the swastika flag in his hand), a photograph taken in Allrode in the Hartz Mountains. It is highly probable that this boy, like thousands of others, joined the ranks of the Waffen-SS in the war.

BELOW: A group of girls from the Bund deutscher Mädel. It was Himmler's wish to set up a Women's Academy for Wisdom and Culture to educate females selected for their intellect, wit, grace of body, political reliability and Germanic appearance. In reality his aim was racial breeding with his SS men.

Below: Hitler with members of the Hitler Youth. Undoubtedly many young Germans who met or saw Hitler before the war were mesmerised by him. One member of the League of German Girls told the author: 'His eyes were rivetting, blue I think, and his personality captivating. When he spoke to me I was tongue-tied.' To get into the Waffen-SS and be part of the Führer's bodyguard was a great achievement, as Eduard Janke, who joined the *Nordland* Division states: 'Why did I volunteer for the Waffen-SS and not the Wehrmacht? Simple – I wanted to serve in an élite formation.'

EMSLAND

The camp at Emsland was one of the first labour camps set up by the Nazis in an effort to combat unemployment. It was later taken over by the SS.

BELOW: An RAD officer at Emsland. The first labour camp was established at Hammerstein in Grenzmark in January 1932, but it was in Anhalt that the RAD made rapid progress in establishing compulsory labour service.

RIGHT: An Emsland officer of the Reichsarbeitsdienst (RAD), Labour Service, on his wedding day in Allrode. His cuff band bears the title 'Anhalt', which was the first region in Germany to make labour service state wide.

LEFT: An RAD recruit at the Emsland camp. He is wearing a greatcoat, no doubt against the cold conditions in the camp. These camps were rudimentary in the extreme; indeed, they were designed as such as part of the 'hardening' process for German males. The six months' labour service law of 26 June 1935 was mandatory for all men between the ages of 19 and 25. The immediate effects of the law was to reduce the unemployment figures, which increased the popularity of the Nazi Party with the voters.

RIGHT: The Emsland camp in winter, a cold and uninviting place. The camp later became a place to house the enemies of National Socialism, though no doubt the appearance of the buildings changed little. Eicke's concentration camp guards often lived in conditions not much better than those of the inmates. As time wore on conditions for the guards improved, while those of the prisoners greatly deteriorated.

RIGHT: The certificate that granted Arbeitsmann Gerhard Frühauf the honour of wearing the Emsland cuff band. Such cuff bands denoted membership of a distinct group, and were prized by their recipients. This was but a part of making individuals feel special, of appealing to their sense of pride. In this way individuals could be moulded to become fervent supporters of the regime, ready to give their lives if necessary for the Führer. Such was the fate of Gerhard Frühauf, younger brother of Carl-Heinz, who was killed in action on the Eastern Front in 1942.

LEFT: The Emsland camp gates, complete with an honour guard of an RAD man. Instead of a rifle he has a spade, as denoting the type of service undertaken in the Labour Service. Men called up for labour service worked mostly in agriculture or public works, while women, who were later included, undertook domestic service and what were called 'traditionally female' agricultural jobs.

RIGHT: The SS-Führersportschan Mihla a. Werra, one of the organisations established within the SS to promote sporting activities. Sport played an important part in the Nazi scheme of things, preparing as it did individuals for the rigours of active war service. Sports training began at the age of 14 for German youths, and went hand-in-hand with military style drill, training exercises and political and racial indoctrination. In the armed SS great emphasis was placed on sport and physical fitness.

LEFT: Members of the SS-Totenkopfverbände read the sports page of the local paper. Note the track suit sporting large SS runes. Intensive physical activity was a large part of life in the Waffen-SS, and thus rations reflected this. Eicke's men lived like fighting cocks: a typical daily menu consisted of coffee, marmalade, bread and sausage for breakfast; meat, potatoes and vegetables for lunch; and coffee, stew, milk and potato salad at the end of the day, all washed down with liberal quantities of tea, beer and, on special occasions, wine. Food was never in short supply for Eicke's men.

RIGHT: SS-Totenkopfverbände members at the end of a day's sporting activity. Throughout the armed SS sport was integral to training, as Hans-Gerhard Starck of the *Leibstandarte* Division states: 'The days spent in training were long and hard. It was repeated until everything was automatic. We were all good at sports, but the instructors always pushed us to the limits of our endurance and gave us tasks to prove our steadfastness.'

RIGHT: Soldiers of the SS-Totenkopfverbände are put through their paces at the Dachau camp. Those responsible for training the SS-Verfügungstruppe, Felix Steiner and Paul Hausser, wanted to create a super fit body of troops. To achieve this, traditional military training was integrated with sport, physical fitness and fieldcraft. Sport was used to engender a spirit of comradeship between individuals in a unit, as well as to create fit soldiers.

BELOW: These SS-Totenkopfverbände members find time to relax at the end of another long day. The music is provided by a harmonica, while the flowers in the vase seem to belie the reputation of SS soldiers as being hardened individuals. Appearances can be deceptive, though: note the austere nature of the men's living quarters. Their commander, Theodor Eicke, was in no doubt as to what made a good SS soldier. In each billet he had a sign erected. It stated: 'Praise be that which toughens.' For him physical and mental toughness were one and the same.

ABOVE: RAD men undertake kit cleaning at the Emsland camp. Cleanliness was an integral part of SS-Verfügungstruppe training. One Waffen-SS soldier, Jan Munk, remembers his days spent in training: 'Cleaning things was something special. If they told you that your room, your rifle or your uniform had to be clean, they meant *clean*. On a Saturday morning we usually had our major cleaning exercise. It started with all the lads on hands and knees scrubbing the long stone corridors and stairs.'

LEFT: Inside the barracks at Dachau. Discipline within the SS-Totenkopfverbände could be severe. One of Eicke's men, for example, tried to resign from the SS-Totenkopfverbände. Eicke had him dressed in the uniform of a prison inmate, paraded before the entire division and then shipped off to Buchenwald concentration camp. The threat of becoming a concentration camp inmate had a powerful effect on Eicke's men, as they lived in the camps and experienced how the inmates were treated first-hand.

ABOVE: Exhausted SS men photographed during a sports contest. SS military training included a strict physical programme: there was always one hour of rigorous exercise each day before breakfast, followed by intensive weapons training, target practice and unarmed combat training. After lunch there would be an intensive drill session, to be followed by cleaning of kit and then a run, or two hours on the sports field. As a result of SS soldiers spending more time on the athletics field and in cross-country running than on the parade ground, they developed high standards of fitness and endurance, such as being able to run 3km (1.6 miles) carrying a full kit load in 20 minutes.

LEFT: Vaulting a mock wall during a cross-country steeple chase. The training programme of Felix Steiner and Paul Hausser soon yielded results: the soldiers of the armed SS were fitter than their army counterparts, and even the *Leibstandarte*, that law unto itself, lagged behind (though Dietrich, seeing the gap develop, soon brought it into line with the rest of the SS-Verfügungstruppe). But it was not just the physical training which set the SS apart. The qualities of its membership was also a factor: high morale, aggressive attitude and a belief that they were a political and military élite. The camaraderie which existed within the armed SS was also important.

LOOKING AFTER ITS OWN

Part of the creed of the Waffen-SS was that it looked after its own. This reinforced the view that it was a closed order with its own set of rules and regulations.

LEFT: The soldier on the right is Jan Munk, a foreign volunteer in the Waffen-SS. After being wounded in action in Russia he was sent to Pörtschach am Wörthersee, west of Klagenfurt, to recuperate. This place was known as an erholungsheim, recuperation home. Originally a high-class holiday resort, during the war it was commandeered by the Wehrmacht. It looked after all sections of the German armed forces, including the Waffen-SS. The other SS soldier is, like Munk, a Dutch volunteer in the service of Germany, while the two in the middle are Austrian mountain troops.

RIGHT: Munk (far left) at Pörtschach. Unflinching obedience, honesty and dedication to duty was expected of all Waffen-SS men. From the very first day of training it was impressed upon individuals that they were part of an élite. Absolute trust in one's comrades was part of the SS creed. Thus lockers in rooms were left unlocked. Part of this creed was that wounded were never left to fall into the hands of the enemy, and individuals like Munk knew that if they were wounded their comrades would do everything in their power to retrieve them, even if it meant sacrificing themselves.

RIGHT: SS barracks near Klagenfurt. This photograph is taken from the back of the staff quarters. The group of low buildings which can be seen housed garages, armoury and quartermaster's stores. SS barracks were different from their army counterparts, as attested to by Heinz Köhne of the *Leibstandarte*: 'In the Wehrmacht one had to keep one's locker secured. In the Waffen-SS they had to be left open. There was no theft in the Waffen-SS.' The motto of the Waffen-SS was 'Loyalty is my Honour'.

LEFT AND BELOW: Two more views of the barracks near Klagenfurt. The view left is the main entrance, while the parade ground with staff quarters in the background is illustrated below. All recruits had to attend indoctrination classes. However, as most members had been members of the Hitler Youth and were supporters of National Socialism anyway, such classes seemed to have been rather superfluous. Indoctrination was much more intense in Eicke's SS-Totenkopfverbände, as was the discipline, though all Waffen-SS soldiers, especially at the beginning of the war, believed that they were the physical embodiment of Nazi values.

ABOVE: SS-Totenkopfverbände recruits in their barracks at Dachau. In October 1939, the camp was cleared of inmates to make way for a large influx of SS men in preparation for the creation of the *Totenkopf* Division, a fully motorised infantry formation. It was to consist of a divisional staff, three motorised infantry regiments, an artillery regiment, a communications battalion, an engineer battalion, a tank-destroyer battalion, a reconnaissance battalion and support units.

LEFT: Peeling potatoes, the bane of soldiers in every army. These RAD boys are undertaking mess duties in their barracks at the Emsland camp. No doubt two of the group are smoking of pipes in order to look more mature. Unquestioning obedience was drilled into SS recruits, which had two effects on the battlefield. One was that Waffen-SS units carried out their orders to the letter, no matter what the consequences; the other was the high casualties suffered by individual units trying to carry out those orders.

LEFT: A group of SS soldiers undertaking weapons cleaning. They are dressed in the first-pattern drill uniform, which comprised a five-buttoned shapeless jacket with stand-up collar and equally shapeless trousers. During the war the Waffen-SS would pioneer the use of disruptive-pattern camouflage clothing, which would later be adopted by all modern armies in Europe and the Americas.

BELOW: Members of the SS-Totenkopfverbände carrying out training in the use of grenades. Live-firing exercises were a part of Waffen-SS training from the start, the idea being to accustom individuals to the noises experienced in battle. Such training inevitably led to fatalities, but undoubtedly saved lives when SS units were called upon to fight on the battlefield.

LEFT: SS-Totenkopfverbände men undertake recognition training at Dachau. The nucleus of the *Totenkopf* Division was formed from the original three concentration camp guard regiments: *Oberbayern*, *Brandenburg* and *Thuringen*. Training was intensive, though the procurement of weapons and equipment proved to be a problem. Exercises in the field involved the whole division, in order to acquaint its personnel with the tenets of mobile warfare.

BELOW: SS-Sturmbannführer der Reserve Carl-Heinz Frühauf (right), who was promoted to SS-Oberscharführer on 9 November 1937. Between November 1937 to June 1938 he held various assignments, such as primary marksmanship instructor. He is seen here in this capacity. One Waffen-SS veteran spoke of weapons training thus: 'Manoeuvres were very realistic, with live ammunition being used on certain exercises, but not before every man knew his weapon and how to take cover.' Each man had to know how to strip and re-assemble his personal weapon, as well as the machine guns in service.

BELOW: Members of the *Leibstandarte* swear their oath of loyalty to their Führer: 'I swear to you, Adolf Hitler, as Führer and Chancellor of the Reich, loyalty and bravery, I promise to you, and those you have appointed to have authority over me, obedience unto death.' Thus was the pact sealed.

BELOW: Inside the Brown House, the Munich Nazi Party headquarters. Here party records and awards were prepared and registered. The building had been built in 1828 and called the Barlow-Palais. However, it had fallen into disrepair and substantial restoration had to be carried out before it could be inhabited by the NSDAP. The Nazis took possession in 1931. The Brown House was grandly decorated, and Hitler had a large and ornate office on the second floor, which was dominated by a painting of Frederick the Great.

CHAPTER FOUR

Baptism of Fire
The SS campaign in Poland, 1939

The SS was party to a deception that gave Hitler the excuse he needed to attack Poland and begin the most destructive war mankind has ever seen. On 30 August 1939, in response to German belligerence, Polish mobilisation was officially announced. Hitler could wait no longer, and so the next day he gave the order to invade Poland at 0445 hours. The time had come to undertake the deception Hitler perceived was necessary to legitimise the invasion. SS-Sturmbannführer Alfred Naujocks was chosen by SS-Obergruppenführer Heydrich to lead the simulated attack on the Gleiwitz radio station. Naujocks was one of the most audacious commanders in the Sicherheitsdienst (SD), the SS Security Department.

DECEPTION AT GLEIWITZ

At 1600 hours on 31 August, SS-Obergruppenführer Heydrich alerted Naujocks at Gleiwitz (the German operational staff of the station, however, were not privy to his plan). Corpses from Dachau concentration camp arrived on lorries, and the dead 'Polish soldiers' were scattered convincingly around the station. The deception party arrived on time and they began making as much noise as possible, hoping to give the impression that the station was under attack by a large Polish insurgent force. The ceiling of the studio received several shots, adding to the bedlam and petrifying the radio station personnel. Then Naujocks' Polish-speaking announcers broadcast anti-German statements to the background accompaniment of shots fired by other SS men for the next five minutes. Having decided they had convinced the listeners that the radio station was under attack by armed Poles, SS-Sturmbannführer Naujocks and his men withdrew. A successful mock attack on the German customs station at

LEFT: SS artillery in action during the Polish Campaign. The artillery piece is a 3.7cm Pak 35/36.

OPPOSITE: The spoils of war. Wehrmacht officers show Hitler a captured ensign of the Polish 8th Horse Rifles Regiment. Second from right is Reichsführer-SS Heinrich Himmler.

Hochlinden was also made. Hitler had his justification for invading Poland (in fact, Hitler's soldiers and tanks were on the move before the SS men had returned to their bases). Hitler sent a message to the German armed forces the same day vowing: 'To put an end to these mad acts I can see no other way but from now onwards to meet force with force.'

THE SS ORDER OF BATTLE FOR POLAND

Himmler had hoped that the armed SS would be used as a single formation during the Polish Campaign, but the SS was divided among army units. The Panzer Division *Kempf* contained the *Deutschland* Regiment, the SS-Aufklärungs Abteilung (Reconnaissance Detachment) and the SS-Nachrichtensturmbann (Signals Company). The division, under the Command of Major-General Werner Kempf, was deployed as part of I Corps in General Fedor von Bock's Army Group North. The 10th Army, under General Walter von Reichenau, contained the *Leibstandarte* and the SS-Pioniersturmbann, while the *Germania* Regiment was retained in reserve in East Prussia as part of the 14th Army. The third SS-Verfügungstruppe Standarte, *Der Führer*, was not fully trained and did not take part in the campaign.

SS-Standartenführer Felix Steiner, leading the *Deutschland* Regiment, struck south in the direction of Mlava under the searing sun and marching through dusty terrain. Initially, despite the difficult conditions, good progress was made.

LEFT: SS officers stand before the crypt of one of Poland's heroes, Marshal Pilsudski, victor of the Battle of Warsaw in 1920. There was to be no saviour for the Poles 19 years later, however. Himmler was determined that the SS should be blooded in Poland: 'The Verfügungstruppe is created to go into the field.'

However, due to fuel shortages its motorised capabilities could not be fully utilised, also the Polish positions were strongly constructed at the approaches to Mlava and manned by determined troops. Polish resistance began to stiffen considerably, and this led to *Deutschland*'s first important engagement. After a heavy and prolonged softening-up barrage by German artillery, which proved less destructive than had been hoped for, the Polish bunker system was still intact. A two-pronged thrust against the Polish hill defences was ordered, which Deutschland undertook, supported by tanks from the 7th Panzer Regiment. The tank attack faltered almost immediately when the vehicles ran into well prepared anti-tank obstacles. The German tanks, mainly light Panzer Is and Panzer IIs, were inadequately armed to breach the defences. Polish artillery knocked out several tanks, and the remaining vehicles pulled back. To make matters worse, the promised Luftwaffe Stuka dive-bomber attacks failed to appear.

HARD FIGHTING ON THE NAREW

Undeterred, SS-Standartenführer Felix Steiner and SS-Standartenführer Matthais Kleinheisterkamp formed SS battle groups, supported by a battle group from the 7th Panzer Regiment. In this new advance the Poles were swiftly driven back all the way to the River Narew. Here they formed new defence lines at Rozan around the network of four old czarist Russian forts. The Poles vigorously defended these positions, losing many men, while the Germans' own losses were considerable. The resistance was strong enough to halt removing the remaining Poles from their positions.

To avoid encirclement, the Poles were forced to evacuate Rozan as farther to the south German forces had crossed the Narew, leaving the Polish success short-lived. The River Bug

had been crossed by the Germans on 10 September in an attempt to prevent Polish units strengthening the defences around Warsaw by withdrawing into the capital. On 16 September, Warsaw was completely encircled when Kleinheisterkamp and his battle group reached the Vistula, closing the ring around the city.

The Polish forts at Modlin and Zacrozym were next to be neutralised. Modlin was a stronghold to be reckoned with, holding approximately 35,000 troops. To take part in the attack, *Deutschland* was moved to the northwest of Warsaw. On 29 September, SS troops stormed Modlin in a final assault, and General Zehak signed the fortress capitulation order at 1450 hours. Zacrozym was then attacked after a concentrated artillery barrage and was captured within 90 minutes, resulting in several thousand Polish prisoners being taken.

GERMANIA'S WAR

During the night of 16-17 August, the *Germania* Regiment, under the command of SS-Standartenführer Carl-Maria Demelhuber, was assembled in preparation for the Polish Campaign, and placed under the command of the 14th Army. Its armoured car platoon was to serve under the 8th Reconnaissance Unit of the 8th Armoured Division. Although *Germania* remained in reserve for most of the four-week war, it was assigned the task of protecting the flank of XXII Army Corps in its drive towards Chelm as part of the 10th Army attacking from Silesia. However, it was spread too thin for the amount of ground it was expected to cover.

The task of blocking the Przemysl-Lemberg road fell to the 15th Company. Here the SS infantry surprised a Polish column and, despite being vastly outnumbered, managed to take over 500 prisoners. Officers and cadets from the Polish War Academy at Kraców, who had been formed into a powerful unit, were attempting to fight their way through to Lemberg on the evening of the same day, ran into the small SS unit. The Germans took heavy casualties and were forced to withdraw to the north to link up with the 1st Company. The SS troops were ordered to hold their positions despite the perilous situation. Przemysl was under attack from the 7th Infantry Division, and the SS soldiers succeeded in stopping any Polish troops from escaping.

The regiment's 2nd Battalion, attached to the 8th Infantry Division in VIII Army Corps, advanced towards the line Brzoza-Stadnice-Linica. At Kreszov there was a vital bridge over the River San which had to be captured. The SS men made an 80km (50-mile) forced march in two days, encountering elements of the 5th Panzer Division en route. The two units advanced, and in the afternoon of 12 September reached the west bank opposite Kreszov. However, as they were preparing to cross the bridge it was blown up. A platoon from 3rd and 5th Companies crossed the river that night, only to find that under the cover of darkness the Poles had withdrawn. The fleeing enemy was pursued by a third company the 6th Company, which came so close to them at times that Stukas harrying the retreat. were in danger of hitting the SS troops. Pushing on, the San's eastern banks had been secured by the time the 8th Infantry Division arrived.

THE *LEIBSTANDARTE* GOES ONTO THE OFFENSIVE

The *Leibstandarte*, commanded by SS-Gruppenführer 'Sepp' Dietrich, together with elements of the SS-Pioniersturmbann, was deployed in the central sector and was assigned the task of protecting the exposed flanks of the Wehrmacht units that were racing ahead.

The 4th Panzer Division advanced towards Lodz, and the *Leibstandarte* was ordered to support it. Initially everything in its path was swept aside easily, but the farther it advanced into the Polish heartland resistance stiffened. In the built-up areas of large towns vicious street fighting often bogged the regiment down, and at Pabianice Polish units surrounded the SS men. The beleaguered *Leibstandarte* was only relieved by the intervention of army troops.

The pincer movement of the 4th and 10th Armies was executed, and to the

RIGHT: The German battleship *Schleswig-Holstein* bombards Polish positions on Westerplatte in early September 1939. This ship, which arrived at Danzig on 25 August 1939 ostensibly on a goodwill visit, was in fact transporting German assault troops, who were hidden below decks.

west of Warsaw vast numbers of Polish troops were cut off as the Germans closed in on the capital. The Germans believed these units would drive east, but they struck south. The *Leibstandarte* was now attached to the 8th Army, and on 10 September these Polish units smashed into its exposed flank. The Poles assaulted the 8th Army's flank for two days until their attacks began to lose their momentum. Finally they had to turn east in the hope of reaching Warsaw. The next move the *Leibstandarte* made was westwards, taking part in the encirclement on the River Bzura.

THE BLITZKRIEG VINDICATED

On 26-27 September Warsaw was shelled and bombed and forced to capitulate. Fighting on the Baltic and Polish shores ended on 1 October when the Polish naval commander surrendered; on 6 October the last Polish troops ceased fighting.

The 36-day war against Poland did not put a serious strain on the German war machine. Germany was seen as having had a marked superiority over Poland in all respects. The assurance of Soviet cooperation was the final nail in Poland's coffin, and even the weather stayed fine. The German armed forces were able to conduct the campaign at lightening speed. The hitherto accepted rate of movement of 24km (15 miles) in 24 hours for military operations was now multiplied several times. The contribution of the SS-Verfügungstruppe was modest but not negligible. The SS-Totenkopfverbände, on the other hand, made no tactical contribution to the German victory, but was extensively involved in the Führer's social plan for Poland.

German casualties, according to their October 1939 estimate, were 8082 killed, 27,279 wounded and 5029 missing, although the final figures were slightly higher. German tank losses were 217 destroyed and a large number damaged, while the Luftwaffe lost 285 aircraft destroyed. Polish casualties were much higher and included civilians.

RIGHT: 1400 hours, 1 September 1939. The German campaign against Poland, codenamed 'Case White', is under way. Here soldiers of the German 7th Infantry Division engage Polish forces dug in near near Wegierska Górka. By the time this photograph was taken the war was nearly 12 hours old, and two German army groups, comprising one and a half million men, were racing across Poland's borders towards Warsaw.

LEFT: Troops of the SS-Heimwehr *Danzig*, an SS home defence force stationed in the demilitarised Free City of Danzig (as established by the Treaty of Versailles). The unit was affiliated to the SS-Totenkopfverbände. During the Polish Campaign it was used to help secure the port and its environs for the Germans. The SS men are moving up to clear a Polish barricade and are supported by an Austrian-built armoured car, one of several dozen such vehicles in German service at this time.

RIGHT: Soldiers of the SS-Heimwehr *Danzig* prepare to attack the post office in Danzig, which was occupied by Polish troops. Despite the valiant attempts of the defenders, the Poles were eventually forced to surrender. Most of them were subsequently shot by the SS troops. It was not the only atrocity it committed: on 8 September it shot 33 Polish civilians in the village of Ksaizki in the province of Pomerania. The men of the SS-Heimwehr *Danzig* were eventually absorbed into the *Totenkopf* Division, and their actions in Poland would have been approved by Theodor Eicke, wrote stated to his officers in the first few days of the war: 'Now in this war the SS has the main task of protecting Adolf Hitler's state, above all from every internal danger.' He believed only the SS possessed the 'hardness' to protect Germany from her enemies, both internally and externally.

RIGHT: The first Polish prisoners begin to make their way west into captivity. The *Leibstandarte*, part of Army Group South, took its first group of prisoners at the town of Boleslavecz on 1 September, after fierce fighting against the Polish 30th Infantry Division, 21st Infantry Regiment and armoured cars of the Wolwyska Cavalry Brigade. Following close-quarter combat the town was taken, and very soon a long line of Polish prisoners were making their way down the road along which the *Leibstandarte* had attacked.

BELOW: The advance continues. The motorised SS units were in great demand during the Polish Campaign, being able to transfer from one point to another quicker than the army's infantry, who for the most part relied on their feet for transport. However, the Polish road network was poor, and as the weather stayed fine the SS found the dust and sand ruined pistons and jammed weapons. When it did rain the roads soon turned into quagmires, into which trucks and armoured cars sank up to their axles. And during the campaign the Germans started to suffer from fuel shortages.

BELOW: An SS light mortar crew in action during the early phase of the Polish Campaign. Note how dry the soil is. Though the heat and dryness were sapping both physically and mentally, they could have advantages. On 2 September, for example, the German 8th Army was able to gets its men and vehicles across the River Prosna without difficulty, as the unusually dry weather had lowered its level. By 3 September the German Blitzkrieg was achieving results: the 10th Army had started to break through north of Chestakova, and two panzer divisions were racing towards Warsaw. The jaws of the German pincer were beginning to close around those Polish armies west of the capital.

ABOVE: Soldiers of the *Leibstandarte* near the small market town of Pabianice in early September 1939. The town was on a road and rail junction on the River Ner and a Polish stronghold. It contained a garrison backed up by artillery, including anti-tank guns. An additional problem faced by the SS soldiers was the great number of enemy marksmen in and around the town. A favoured tactic they used was to hide in trees and shoot at lone motorcyclists or staff cars. In reply, the SS peppered trees and bushes with rifle grenades. In addition, as this part of Poland was cultivated with large areas of sunflowers and maize, the SS soldiers had to stalk Polish infantry in small groups among the tall plants.

ABOVE: A final weapons check for this *Leibstandarte* soldier before the assault on Pabianice begins. On 7 September the 1st and 2nd Companies went in, supported by mortar and artillery fire. Despite intensive machine-gun and artillery fire, the SS soldiers managed to breach the Polish first line of defence.

RIGHT: Polish dead outside Pabianice. The Poles always fought with great tenacity during the campaign, and at Pabianice forced the *Leibstandarte* back through the town on 7 September. The SS troops stabilised their positions, however, and after repulsing a fanatical enemy charge in the late afternoon, captured the town.

BELOW: Soldiers of the SS-Heimwehr *Danzig* move through trees smashed by artillery and small-arms fire during the fighting for Westerplatte. They were backed up by German police and SA units from Danzig, plus naval infantry off-loaded from the *Schleswig-Holstein.*

RIGHT: Members of the *Deutschland* Regiment near Modlin on 19 September. The forts at Modlin, to the north-west of Warsaw, had to be taken if the Polish capital was to fall to the Germans. The investment of the forts lasted from 19 to 28 September, and Steiner had to wait until the 22nd until he could send out patrols to probe the enemy.

BELOW: *Deutschland's* light artillery pounds Zacrozym Fort in late September. The attack on the fort was made on 29 September with infantry and flamethrowing detachments, and after fierce fighting the defences were breached and the fort taken. Fort No 1 was also taken, ending the *Deutschland* Regiment's war in Poland.

BELOW RIGHT: Soldiers of the *Leibstandarte* fighting in Sochaczev in mid-September 1939. The fighting for this town was particularly bitter, being part of the wider German effort to destroy a large pocket of enemy troops. At Sochaczev the last commander of the garrison was a private, all officers and NCOs having ben killed.

LEFT: SS soldiers evacuate a wounded comrade. The SS's intensive pre-war training had reaped dividends in Poland, and in general Himmler's troops had exceeded all expectations. Though SS training was realistic, the reality of war struck even the élite of the Third Reich. A *Leibstandarte* soldier wrote of the area between Modlin and Warsaw: 'The whole area was a scene of death and destruction. The bloated bodies of men and animals blackening under the hot sun, smashed carts, burnt-out vehicles and those most tragic victims of war, the wounded horses, waiting for the mercy shot.'

LEFT: A *Leibstandarte* soldier edges forward near Sladov during the final phase of the fighting in Poland. By this time the Polish Army was disintegrating under relentless Luftwaffe and artillery attack. The Polish Army had been smashed along the River Bzura. All that was left as September neared its end was the capture of Warsaw itself.

RIGHT: Keeping watch for the enemy. But for these SS soldiers in late September 1939 the fight is over. Poland has been convincingly beaten, her armies suffering at least 66,000 killed and 200,000 wounded, with a further 694,000 taken prisoner.

ABOVE: On 25 September 1939, Hitler, accompanied by Himmler, visited detachments of the *Leibstandarte* and inspected the 13th Company encamped near Guzov. When the campaign ended his bodyguard was ordered to move to Prague, where it received a rapturous reception and its men were granted leave. The *Leibstandarte* had fought well in Poland, and justifiably earned the praise of Hitler. The decision to include the armed SS in the war had been vindicated.

LEFT: Hitler with 'Sepp' Dietrich during the same inspection. The armed SS had suffered proportionately much higher casualties than the army during the Polish Campaign, which prompted the Army High Command to express negative views about the SS-Verfügungstruppe. It held the view that it had not ben trained properly for the war, and in particular its officer corps was found wanting. For their part, SS commanders complained that their units were fragmented and given especially difficult missions. There was probably some truth in both views.

RIGHT: An SS soldier is decorated in the field during the Polish Campaign. Despite the view of the German High Command regarding the armed SS, individual German Army commanders often had nothing but praise for Himmler's troops. Major-General Kempf described the *Deutschland* Regiment thus: 'It is in all respects a fully capable infantry regiment commanded [by SS-Standartenführer Felix Steiner] with great circumspection.' Kempf reserved special praise for the regiment's signals units, whose achievements were 'at an exemplary level I have never before experienced'. Later in the war many German Army commanders were to express such sentiments about SS units.

BELOW: The German victory parade in Warsaw. For Himmler the inclusion of the SS-Verfügungstruppe in the war had been crucial in order for it to gain credibility, as he himself stated to his subordinates just before the war: 'If I designate the total task of the SS ... as guaranteeing the internal security of Germany, then it is only possible to perform this task if a part of the SS stands at the front and bleeds. Were we to bring no blood sacrifice and were not to fight at the front, we would lose the moral obligation to shoot people who sneak home and are cowardly. That is the reason for the SS-Verfügungstruppe, which has the very noblest task, to be permitted to go into the field.'

CHAPTER FIVE

On Parade

The ceremonial face of the Waffen-SS

World War I produced radical social changes within Germany. Hundreds of thousands of men, most of whom had previously never been away from their village or town, had returned from the horrors of the front. For their sacrifice they wished for better things for themselves and their families. But Germany had been defeated, her armies disbanded and her soldiers forbidden to wear their uniforms and old awards. This naturally caused resentment, and the later economic privations caused by the reparations of the Versailles Treaty and the worldwide economic depression, created a massive pool of disaffected individuals who had little faith in the government of the Weimar Republic. The Nazi Party was but one of the fringe parties in Germany that tapped into this manpower pool, but it was one of the most successful. It's paramilitary organisations in particular, the SA and SS, offered its members, most of whom had been in the army during the war, the life for which they yearned. Nazi Party leaders saw the resurrection of ceremonies, pageantry, awards and massed rallies as the means by which they could recreate the state of Germany in the Nazi mould.

THE WAFFEN-SS ON PARADE

The ceremonial face of the Waffen-SS had its origins in the birth, on 17 March 1933, of a new Headquarters Guard named the SS Stabswache *Berlin*. The unit initially comprised 120 hand-picked volunteers, of whom some were former members of the *Stosstrupp Adolf Hitler*, and which became the SS Sonderkommando *Zossen* two months later. As well as the guard duties, it could also be employed for anti-terrorist and armed police activities. At the Parteitag des Siegers (Victor's Party Rally) on 31 August 1933 to mark the Nazi

LEFT: A column of panzers pass through crowd-lined streets in Nuremberg in 1935. Military displays were used to portray an image of a strong Germany to her people.

OPPOSITE: Huge swastikas form the backdrop for Hitler and Himmler at the 1935 Party Day Rally. As ever, his black SS guards are present.

accession to power, Hitler formally recognised the *Adolf Hitler* SS-Standarte, and by late 1933 the *Leibstandarte* was garrisoned at Berlin-Lichterfelde. Here, its ceremonial duties included forming the Reich Chancellery guard, as well as other state and party functions, where it held the place of honour at the end of the parade. Its duties were further expanded to encompass all walks of Hitler's life. Its members served as adjutants, waiters, general servants and drivers. Members of the *Leibstandarte* guarded the entrance to the new Reich Chancellery, Hitler's palatial Berlin headquarters, completed in January 1939. In keeping with the image of the new Germany, the SS guards stood vigil in black parade uniforms, complete with white belts, cross-straps, ammunition pouches, bayonet frogs and gloves.

NEW UNIFORMS AND AWARDS

The best designers, jewellers and artists found favour and patronage under the National Socialists, and were commissioned to create the awards for the new uniforms that abounded as Germany became militarised. It was a revival of some of the lost splendour and tradition of the old Germany, a revival of the old standards and styles under the colours of the new regime. Hitler understood the sense of pride and importance that was engendered when a man was uniformed and bedecked with medals proclaiming his bravery in battle or duty to the party. Thus glittering decorations began to adorn the chests of the new statesmen of the Reich. Paradoxically, Hitler himself wore few decorations, only his Iron Cross and wound badge earned in World War I, and his Golden Party Badge and Blood Order of his National Socialist Party. His appearance contrasted sharply with that of medal-festooned cronies such as Göring and Ribbentrop at the various state and party rallies. This was a clever ploy: the plain aspect of his uniform and the notable absence of decorations suggested some identity with the common man. However, Hitler's personal quirk in not adorning himself with decorations did not preclude him from constantly reviewing and approving new designs, and using formal occasions to award them. For his part, Himmler was determined to bring about a Black Holy Order built on the myths conjured up in his furtive imagination. This order was to be a brotherhood which was spiritually descended from the heroes of pagan and medieval Germany.

The German calendar was changed to honour the ceremonial landmarks of the New Order: 30 January was celebrated as the date of coming to power; 20 April, Hitler's birthday, became a day of national tribute; 1 May – May Day – was now renamed 'Day of National Labour'; and the summer solstice was revived. The highlight of the National Socialist calendar, however, was the Nuremberg Rally, or Parteitag, which was held each year in September. On 9 November, the anniversary of the Munich Putsch, the survivors silently re-enacted their march through the streets of the Bavarian capital, led by its venerated cadre.

The SS attempted to replace the individual family anniversaries and Christian rites of marriage, christening and death, with neo-pagan ones, with Christmas being celebrated on 21 December, the winter solstice, and called Julfest. This was the climax of the year in Himmler's scheme of events, and brought SS members together at candlelit banquet tables and around raging bonfires that were reminiscent of German tribal rituals. At each place was set wine, a loaf of bread and in some cases a special yuletide candle holder.

The role of pageantry and uniform, combined with the aspects of medals and decorations, fitted in well with Nazi ideology and the almost theatrical splendour of dressing up for occasions of state. Hitler and Göbbels staged massive rallies involving often over 100,000 people at a time at every conceivable occasion. The sixth Parteitag held in 1934 was called 'Triumph of the Will' and was the largest to date. Its mixture of medieval pageant and scout jamboree made an enormous impression, not only on the German participants but also on the spectators, who included many invited foreigners. The high point of these meetings was the consecration of new colours and standards. Hitler ceremonially held them in one hand while clasping the Blutfahne, the bullet-riddled flag which had allegedly been soaked in the blood of the Nazi martyrs who fell during the Munich Putsch, in the other. It was seen as an act that transmitted the magical essence of the old sacred relic, through Hitler's, to the new standards.

THE NAZI STATE ON DISPLAY

In addition to the annual rallies held at Nuremberg up to 1939, other occasions honouring the armed forces, SA and SS were opportunities to flaunt Germany's military strength, both real and imaginary. They were an opportunity to display public support for the Nazi Party to foreigners, as well as to intimidate those Germans who were opposed to the regime. Filmed for newsreels and broadcast on radio, they were seen and heard throughout Germany and subsequently all over Europe and America. They both frightened Germany's enemies and encouraged her supporters. These rallies and ceremonial events were increasingly marshalled and policed by the Allgemeine-SS, indicating the growing importance that it was acquiring under Himmler's tutelage.

LEFT: Every major rally was an opportunity to display the Blood Banner, that most sacred of Nazi standards. It was ritually paraded before the massed ranks of the Nazis' paramilitary units, as here at Nuremberg in 1935, before being taken to the Führer podium to stand beside Hitler.

The Reichsführer-SS set about implementing his theories to bring about a racially and ideologically élite. In December 1931, for example, the SS introduced its marriage laws. The SS man and his intended bride had to prove Aryan ancestry back to 1800 (1750 for leaders). Marriages no longer took place in churches but in the open under a lime tree, or in an SS building decorated with fir twigs, sunflowers and life runes. An eternal flame burned in an urn, in front of which the couple exchanged rings and received the official SS gift of bread and salt, symbols of the earth's bounty and purity.

At christenings the child was wrapped in a shawl of undyed wool embroidered with oakleaves, runes, and swastikas. Both parents placed their hands on the child's head and pronounced his or her name. The official SS gift for the first child was a blue silk shawl, silver beaker and spoon. For every fourth child the mother received a silver candlestick with the legend, 'you are only a link in the clan's endless chain'.

THE ROUND TABLE AT WEWELSBURG

The castle of Wewelsburg was rebuilt at immense expense as a shrine to Germanic civilisation. Here the Black Holy Order of the SS was founded, and from 1934 held ceremonies several times a year. Karl Wolff, Himmler's adjutant, ushered each SS leader into a monastic cell, where he steeped himself in Germanic mysticism surrounded by treasures from ancient Germany. Beneath their mock medieval coats of arms, the leading 12 high SS officers were assigned places around an Arthurian round table. On the death of any of the members his emblem was to be incinerated in the pit of the Supreme Leaders' Hall and the ashes placed in an urn, which was to stand on one of the twelve pedestals that ringed it. Himmler started a ceramics works in Dachau which produced fine porcelain as well as earthenware. A Damascus smithy was also established which produced official SS gifts and ceremonial items. SS musicians revived the blowing of ancient northern German lurs, performing at Norse music festivals and other special occasions.

Among all the symbolism and regalia of the Black Order was one potent symbol: the Totenkopf (Death's Head). Of all SS uniform trappings, it was this which endured throughout the history of the organisation. It was not adopted simply to strike fear into those who saw it, but was chosen as an emotional link with the past, in particular with the élite military units of Imperial Germany. The other symbols of SS ceremony were the 1933-pattern dagger, which could be worn by all members. The 1936 chained dagger was worn only by officers and by those Old Guard NCO's and other ranks who had joined prior to 30 January 1933. In recognition of exemplary achievement, Himmler presented a Special Honour Dagger. He bestowed upon selected Allgemeine-SS commanders and graduates of the Waffen-SS officer schools at Bad Tölz and

ABOVE: SS-Standartenführer Jakob Grimminger, the man who carried the revered Blood Banner. He took part in the Munich Putsch and was appointed the standard bearer of the banner. To carry the spiritual icon of the Nazi Party, akin to a religious icon, was an honour indeed.

Braunschweig the Reichsführer's Sword of Honour. Still more prodigious were the Birthday swords, awarded to SS generals and other dignitaries as birthday presents.

The sword and dagger were integral parts of Nazi and SS culture, to such an extent that, in a clear attempt to strengthen his hold on the veteran membership, Ernst Röhm issued an order on 3 February 1934 authorising all SA and SS leaders and subordinates who were members prior to 31 December 1931, and who were still members, to receive and wear a specially inscribed Honour Dagger. Röhm's dedication was inscribed on the reverse of the blade. The inscription 'in cordial comradeship Ernst Röhm' was acid etched onto the blade from a template bearing Röhm's own hand writing. After his execution, Himmler awarded 2000 SS Honour Daggers to those who had taken part in the Röhm Purge. By such symbols as rallies, awards and specially awarded swords and daggers did Hitler and Himmler create a mystique around National Socialism, which intoxicated a nation.

FROM THE CRADLE TO THE GRAVE

The SS encompassed every aspect of a member's life, from the moment when he entered the world to his funeral. And Himmler even tried to create his own religion.

RIGHT: An Allgemeine-SS NCO on his wedding day, pictured in Allrode in the Hartz Mountains. Note there are no visible signs of Christianity. This was deliberate, for Himmler was determined to create a cultural framework to replace Christianity. He believed it was the 'age of the final showdown with Christianity', which he was determined to win.

RIGHT: Massed flags of the Hitler Youth are carried past Nazi military officers and various political dignitaries. Membership of the Hitler Youth was a stepping stone to SS membership, which for the ideologically motivated youngsters meant hopefully joining the Waffen-SS. The end result of this was the creation of the 12th SS Panzer Division *Hitlerjugend* during World War II, which fought with great tenacity in Normandy in 1944, suffering up to 80 per cent losses.

LEFT: An SS officer places his hands on a newborn at an SS christening ceremony, though to be correct it should be termed a name-giving rite. This was performed in front of an altar adorned with a portrait of Adolf Hitler. The ceremony is being administered by members of the 33rd SS Regiment *Darmstadt*. Curiously, Himmler believed that such ceremonies should be held in private. This in part was to avoid the new ceremonies being ridiculed by those who were not members of the SS and did not understand them.

RIGHT: The draped coffin of a fallen SS soldier is guarded by members of his unit. Like marriages, funerals were tailored to suit Nazi ideology, particularly by Himmler's notions about the Aryan-Nordic race. This was because, in his own words, 'all the festivals, all the celebrations in human life, in our life, whose Christian forms we cannot accept inwardly, which we can no longer be a party to'. The answer lay, so he thought, in German mysticism.

LEFT: Two soldiers of the *Flandern* Legion stand guard at the grave of SS-Onderstormleider August Schollen while his widow pays her respects. The funeral was held in Brussels on 8 December 1942. Schollen himself was born on 11 September 1915 and during World War II commanded the first regiment of the SS in Flanders. He was killed in Brussels by the resistance on 4 December 1942. The Flemish SS propaganda machine went into overdrive to create a martyr like Horst Wessel.

RIGHT: SS runes surmount the Nazi national war flag at this SS cemetery in Russia during World War II. Remembering one's ancestors and the past was an important part of SS, and Waffen-SS, ritual. Himmler stated: 'A Volk that honours its ancestors will always have children; only those Völker who know no ancestors are childless.'

ABOVE: Josef Tiso, president of a theoretically independent Slovakia, is greeted by an SS guard of honour on his arrival in Berlin. The reality was that Slovakia was a German vassal state, and had no independent foreign policy. The black-uniformed members of the *Leibstandarte* were a familiar sight for foreign diplomats who visited Hitler and Germany before and during the war.

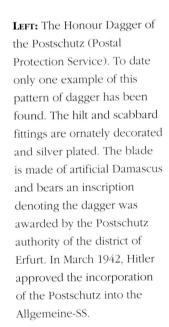

LEFT: The Honour Dagger of the Postschutz (Postal Protection Service). To date only one example of this pattern of dagger has been found. The hilt and scabbard fittings are ornately decorated and silver plated. The blade is made of artificial Damascus and bears an inscription denoting the dagger was awarded by the Postschutz authority of the district of Erfurt. In March 1942, Hitler approved the incorporation of the Postschutz into the Allgemeine-SS.

RIGHT: The castle at Wewelsburg, which was built between 1603 and 1609 in the style of the Weser Renaissance. Its location, on a limestone rock overlooking the Alme valley, plus its shape and history, aroused the interest of Heinrich Himmler. In 1933 the SS rented the castle for one Reichmark per annum, and Himmler put in motion his plans for combining SS ideology with a pseudo-scientific foundation centre. At Wewelsburg Himmler created a Germanic Camelot, where his higher leaders could immerse themselves in mysticism. Himmler's plans for the castle were grandiose, and a concentration camp was established at Wewelsburg to provide slave labour for the planned construction work. Some 1285 of the 3900 inmates died during the building works.

LEFT: The moment all SS men waited for: the award of the SS Dagger. Thousands of these daggers were made during the Third Reich. The presentation of edged weapons (swords and daggers) was used by Hitler and Himmler as a means of expressing gratitude or appreciation. So many blades of one sort or another were authorised for the party and military that it helped the German cutlery industry out of recession. Swords and daggers were also symbols of Nazism and Himmler's SS.

RIGHT: Officers of the *Leibstandarte.* Note the swords hanging from their belts. The officers of the *Leibstandarte* commissioned a special presentation sword for 'Sepp' Dietrich, their commander, its Damascus blade being inscribed with all their names. Damascus blades were the product of a highly complicated process, and Himmler established a Damascus blade school at Dachau concentration camp from 1939 onwards to produce these swords. They were highly prized gifts among the SS.

ABOVE: Hitler and Himmler in front of massed ranks of Deutschland Erwache standards at the Nuremberg rally of 1935. At these rallies the militarised SS units, especially the *Leibstandarte*, wore the distinctive black uniform which fitted in with Himmler's image of the SS as a knightly order. It was both attractive and sinister, and carried awards and distinctions which set the wearer apart from the others. The death's head insignia was symbolic of the SS spirit of loyalty unto death, while the SS runes worn by Waffen-SS soldiers on their right collars denoted the lightning flashes of victory as well as standing for the organisation to which they belonged. Of course the black uniform was impractical for everyday wear, thus from 1937 it began to be replaced by a field-grey uniform similar to that worn by the army.

RIGHT: Hitler on the Führer podium at Nuremberg takes the tribute as SS units and their standards mount the podium to form the back-drop to the rally. Though Hitler knew how to use large rallies, he poured scorn on Himmler's attempts to mythologise the SS: 'What nonsense! Here we have at last reached an age that has left all mysticism behind it, and now he wants to start all over again. We might have just as well have stayed with the church. To think that I may some day be turned into an SS saint!'

LEFT: Hitler reviews massed torch-carrying members of the SA during a night-time parade. Massed rallies during the evening were used effectively by the Nazis to create an aura of power.

RIGHT: Hitler consecrates a new SS Deutschland Erwache standard. Before the war Himmler had boasted that 'I will have no one in my *Leibstandarte* who is not of the best Germany can offer'. Indeed, 'until 1936 we did not accept a man in the *Leibstandarte* if he had even one filled tooth. We were able to assemble the most magnificent manhood in that early Waffen-SS'. And that manhood was on display at each party rally, conveying an image of the SS of superiority and élite soldiers. This was the intention, and invariably helped recruitment.

LEFT: Hitler and his generals take the salute in Vienna after the Austrian *Anschluss* in March 1938. Armed units of the SS took part in the invasion: the *Leibstandarte*, *Deutschland* and *Germania* Regiments. Soon after the invasion a new SS-Verfügungstruppe unit was raised in Vienna, entitled the *Der Führer* Regiment. The invasion, though an easy victory for Hitler, gave the SS-Verfügungstruppe valuable experience of a proper wartime mobilisation.

ABOVE: Music played a very important part in SS pageantry and training; indeed, such was the prestige attached to it in the SS that some of Himmler's units achieved a high level of expertise. The band of the *Leibstandarte*, for example, played at many occasions, such as outside the Chancellery on the occasion of Hitler's birthday. Under its charismatic director of music, Hermann Müller-John, the band became one of the best in the whole of Germany.

LEFT: The *Leibstandarte* on parade, preceded by its famous band. At the band's head is the Schellenbaum, or Jingling Johnny. This particular piece of equipment varied considerably from one unit to another. It could either be a modified imperial piece or one newly assembled, incorporating an eagle, star, half-moon and horse tails. Regulations stated that because of its weight and size, it should be carried by a suitably athletic NCO to prevent it swaying during parades and rallies.

RIGHT: A mounted band of the German Army, complete with kettledrums displaying the imperial drum covers, at a mass rally in Germany before the war. It was from such displays that the SS, especially the *Leibstandarte*, which had its own highly regarded military band, took its lead in the design of instruments. Reichsführer-SS Himmler knew full well the importance of marching songs, and the heart-stirring emotions invoked by a military song, and made sure the SS had its own bands.

BELOW: In stark contrast to the band of the *Leibstandarte*, this motley collection of individuals at Dachau also symbolises the importance the Nazis attached to music. For Himmler everything was geared to achieving what Hans Juttner described as 'a tightly knit aristocracy of manhood, whose special service to the Führer combines with the strongest of SS and military ideals to create a perfect political fighting machine'. However trite it may seem, military music and music from the works of Wagner contributed towards creating the mystique of the SS.

THE SS BROTHERHOOD

The unique entry qualifications, combined with arduous training and a rigid code of conduct, helped to create a closed and exclusive brotherhood of warriors.

RIGHT: Waffen-SS volunteers swear their oath of loyalty to their Führer, Adolf Hitler, over an SS Honour Sword. A solemn occasion full of mystical rites, it assumed the nature of a religious ceremony.

LEFT: Three views of the Totenkopf ring awarded to Willi Raum on Hitler's birthday in 1937. As can be seen, it carried certain symbols such as the death's head and the swastika, the ancient symbol of eternity. The swastika also symbolised the Gibor Rune, which denoted 'Gib' (give) and 'Or' (descendant), and was used as a blessing for the prosperity and survival of the Germanic race. The circle containing the SS runes and arrow symbolised the Tyr, the God of War and Ol, the spirit.

LEFT: Men of the *Leibstandarte* swear their allegiance over an infantry standard in Prague. Though he despised the Catholic church, Himmler had built his SS organisation on the principles of the Order of the Jesuits, and on the dictates as laid down by Ignatius Loyola: absolute obedience was the supreme rule, each and every order had to be obeyed without question. This spirit was enshrined in the SS motto, Loyalty is my Honour, and would form the basis of the Waffen-SS's actions during World War II.

BELOW: The *Leibstandarte* and senior SS officers in Prague. On the eve of World War II the armed SS had been moulded by training and indoctrination into a highly motivated formation. Its ethos was expressed by 'Sepp' Deitrich: 'We ask for and give complete loyalty to the Führer and to those he has set above us. To you recruits I say that even the smallest wish expressed by one of your NCOs must be interpreted as an order from the Führer. Every SS man, therefore, is prepared to carry out unhesitatingly any order issued by the Führer or a superior, regardless of the sacrifice involved.'

CHAPTER SIX

Blitzkrieg in the West

The campaign in the Low Countries and France

There is no evidence to show that Hitler, despite the difficulties he was experiencing with his generals regarding the attack in the West, was considering an expansion of the Waffen-SS at the Wehrmacht's expense after the Polish Campaign. The forthcoming campaign was his primary concern during the winter of 1939-40. An operation involving more than 100 divisions meant the handful of SS troops available were of minor significance. In addition, during the early war years Hitler's attitude towards the armed SS (now officially called Waffen-SS) was still conditioned by his concept of its peacetime role.

After the war Waffen-SS troops would return to their primary role of 'state policemen'. Hitler regarded them in their temporary wartime role as 'guardsmen', while the army constituted the 'troops of the line'. He considered it 'a good thing that the SS should constitute in relation to the others an absolutely distinct world', and the Waffen-SS had a paramount duty to 'set an example'. However, to maintain 'a very high level, the SS shouldn't extend its recruiting too much'.

PLANS FOR 'CASE YELLOW'

The German High Command worked diligently throughout the winter and spring of 1939-40 to prepare the Wehrmacht for 'Case Yellow', the planned offensive in western Europe. The German Army now had a total of 10 panzer divisions with the formation of four new armoured divisions, which were employed for the vitally important mobile spearhead of the Blitzkrieg.

The Wehrmacht was under strength with regard to support for the armoured forces, only having the four motorised infantry divisions it had possessed the previous September

LEFT: Hitler in his command car undertakes a tour of northern France after her defeat, June 1940. Before the campaign in the West he had assured his generals: 'Never again trench warfare.'

OPPOSITE: After France's defeat a German soldier stands before the statue of André Maginot, whose defensive system was bypassed by the Germans.

when the war began. The SS-Verfügungsdivision, *Totenkopf* Division and the reinforced regiment *Leibstandarte SS Adolf Hitler* were thus employed to make up the shortfall. By this time the Waffen-SS had more than 125,000 men in uniform, including the personnel of the SS-Totenkopf regiments, the non-motorised *Polizei* Division and replacements in training.

THE WAFFEN-SS DEPLOYS FOR THE ASSAULT

The SS field formations were deployed in various army corps along Germany's western frontier. Himmler did not object when the *Polizei* Division was assigned a passive defence role opposite the French Maginot Line in 1940. He held no pretensions about it as it was not comprised of SS men, though the Ordnungspolizei had officially been part of the SS since 1936. The concentration camp guards, that much-maligned body of men, was another matter, however. Himmler saw an opportunity to demonstrate that the *Totenkopf* Division was as capable of engaging in the profession of soldiering as the dreaded death's head units were of brutalising helpless prisoners. Himmler considered this a matter of honour, which made him press strongly for the inclusion of the *Totenkopf* Division in the first-wave attack.

Under army command, SS personnel for the first time were required to salute 'according to military and not former

SS or police rank', and were made subject to military regulations. A milestone in the development of the Waffen-SS had arrived, when Himmler's troops fought for the first time in SS divisional formations under the command of their own officers. The combat forces of the SS were at full strength by the end of April 1940 and, despite some shortages in artillery and transport, were ready for battle.

LIGHTNING STRIKES

The German plan in the West involved three main attacks by about 75 divisions, with 45 held in reserve. The objective of the northern-most attack was to crush the Dutch defences and occupy Holland. Dutch airfields would then be denied to the British Royal Air Force (RAF). This was to be delivered by a section of Army Group B, while the remaining and much more powerful portion of the army group was to push into the heart of Belgium. It was hoped that the result of the two attacks would be to lure the allies northward. Army group A would deliver the main German strike, thrusting an armoured wedge through southern Belgium and Luxemburg and into northern France. The Dutch and Belgian Armies would be swept aside if all went according to plan, and the encirclement and destruction of the British Expeditionary Force and a portion of the French Army would then be achieved. Once this was assured Fall Rot ('Case Red') would be implemented: a southward movement of all German forces into France to crush the remainder of the French Army.

When the final dispositions were completed, the *Leibstandarte* and *Der Führer* Regiment, now detached

BELOW: French aircraft destroyed on the ground by the Luftwaffe at Le Bourget airfield. An essential part of the Blitzkrieg was the establishment of German air superiority, after which enemy land units could be subjected to air attack.

from the SS-Verfügungsdivision, stood poised on the Dutch frontier as part of the first wave of the 18th Army in Army Group B. The remainder of the SS-Verfügungsdivision was on alert near Münster, ready to move into Holland as soon as the border defences had been breached. The *Totenkopf* was held in reserve near Kassel, and the *Polizei* Division was in reserve at Tübingen behind the Upper Rhine front of Army Group C. The Waffen-SS was tasked with seizing rail and road bridges over the Dutch border. A second wave encompassing the remainder of the SS-Verfügungsdivision was tasked with forcing crossings over the Dutch border, but farther south.

On 10 May 1940, the *Leibstandarte* overpowered the Dutch border guards and stormed across the border, and by midday had covered 100km (62 miles) and captured Zarolle, where it discovered the Dutch Army had demolished the bridge. Undeterred, the SS troops constructed improvised rafts to cross the River Yssel; they then pushed forward a farther 80km (50 miles) that day. Two major bridges had been successfully blown up by the Dutch, but this obstacle was quickly overcome. On the drive towards Rotterdam the *Leibstandarte* then turned south to link up with elements of the SS-Verfügungsdivision.

THE *TOTENKOPF* GETS A BLOODY NOSE

The sheer size of the German breakthrough and the surprising speed of the advances on 15-16 May startled even senior German commanders, and dictated the call-up of reserves to fill the gaps and protect the flanks of the rapidly widening armoured salient. Accordingly the *Totenkopf* Division was ordered out of the reserve and into action.

On 16 May the *Totenkopf* Division was assigned to General Hoth's XV Panzer Corps, which formed the northern cutting edge of the German spearhead as part of Army Group A. Just before dawn on 18 May Eicke, the division's commander, led the *Totenkopf* to war. As the division motored west on its advance through Holland and then into Belgium, Eicke's columns encountered no enemy resistance, for by 18 May the British and French had been pushed much farther to the west by Bock's Army Group.

However, on 21 May a force of around 74 British tanks and two battalions of infantry, supported by an additional 60 tanks belonging to the French 3rd Light Mechanised Division, slammed into the flanks of the advancing 7th Panzer and *Totenkopf* Division. Eicke succeeded in stalling the tank attack by firing over open sights on the British with 8.8 cm anti-aircraft guns deployed in the anti-tank role. These were the only guns capable of destroying a Matilda at the time. The *Totenkopf* Division suffered high casualties, which resulted in corps commander General Erich Höpner examining the situation at close hand. Höpner held strong professional feelings of opposition and doubts about the *Totenkopf* Division's reliability. Eicke told Höpner that losses made no difference when one held a position and the SS did not retreat in the face of the enemy. Höpner, visibly angered, replied to Eicke by reprimanding him in front of his own staff, accusing him of caring nothing for the lives of his men, and even allegedly calling him a 'butcher' to his face.

By 24 May the *Leibstandarte*, attached to the 1st Panzer Division, was in position near the Aá Canal and poised for the push on Dunkirk when news of Hitler's 'halt order' arrived. The order was lifted on the night of 26-27 May. At Bethune the *Totenkopf* Division crossed the canal and advanced towards Merville. It met determined British resistance, and suffered many casualties.

By early June 1940, though, British and French forces in the north had been pushed back to Dunkirk, where they were evacuated. All three German army groups now turned south. Army Group B advanced on a line from the River Aisne to the coast, Army Group A from the Franco-German border to the River Aisne, and Army Group C attacked through the Maginot Line. Just 65 French formations were arrayed against approximately 140 German divisions. On 5 June Army Group B, including Panzer Group *Kleist*, with the *Leibstandarte* and SS-Verfügungsdivision attached, began its drive towards Paris.

THE BATTLE OF FRANCE

Encountering only light resistance, the SS-Verfügungsdivision had crossed the River Somme by 6 June. On 10 June the French Government abandoned Paris, which was declared an open city two days later. The Meuse was crossed at Château-Thierry by the *Leibstandarte* on 12 June, while the *Totenkopf* Division was released from the reserve to participate in the advance. Hitler ordered 'a sharp pursuit' in the direction of Orlèans to prevent the French from forming a new front south of Paris, while along the eastern front he ordered the 'annihilation' of the remaining French forces. To prevent any French units attempting to escape to the southwest, Panzer Group *Kleist* pushed through the Champagne region towards Dijon.

ABOVE: A well camouflaged 8.8cm German gun fires on retreating British units during the advance to the English Channel in May 1940. The daring German assaults through Holland, Belgium and the Ardennes deceived the Allies and pinned their northern units against the sea.

The motorised *Leibstandarte* was able to keep up with the spearhead of the advance, while the mopping-up operations were carried out by slower divisions which followed in its wake. On 21 June, in the deepest German penetration of the campaign, the *Leibstandarte* marched on St. Etienne, where its garrison surrendered. On the right flank the *Totenkopf* Division had even less to do, though its reconnaissance squadron did fight a furious battle with French colonial troops at Tarare, taking 6000 prisoners.

A general cease-fire went into effect on 25 June 1940. The campaign in the West was over. The *Leibstandarte*, still positioned near St. Etienne, began its journey towards Paris to participate in the great victory parade. The overall performance of the Waffen-SS had delighted Hitler, who once again expressed his unequivocal support. There was no doubt that Himmler's troops had won their spurs. However, military success had been marred by the all too familiar crop of atrocities against prisoners; the dual aspects of high valour and murderous actions would continue until the end of the war.

RIGHT: SS-Obersturmbann-führer Fritz Knöchlein, *Totenkopf* Division. During the campaign in the West in 1940 he commanded the 2nd SS-Totenkopf Regiment's 3rd Company, which on 27 May was engaged in heavy fighting against men of the 2nd Royal Norfolk Regiment near the village of Le Paradis. Around 100 of the British soldiers had barricaded themselves into a farmhouse, from where they managed to pin down Knöchlein's men for nearly an hour with rifle and machine-gun fire, killing and wounding several Waffen-SS soldiers. When the defenders ran out of ammunition and decided to surrender, they showed a white flag, laid down their weapons and marched out of the building. Knöchlein, his temper roused to fury by the audacity of the British soldiers, had them searched, then marched across the road

into a barnyard. They were then put up against a wall and raked with fire from two heavy machine guns. Knöchlein then detailed a squad to bayonet and shoot in the head any who were left alive. After an hour he was satisfied that all were dead, and so ordered his company to resume the advance. Miraculously, two of the British soldiers had survived – Privates Albert Pooley and William O'Callaghan – and it was their testimony after the war which resulted in Knöchlein being hanged by the British in 1949. The incident at Le Paradis was a by-product of the spirit of fanaticism that had been encouraged in the *Totenkopf* Division by its commander, Theodor Eicke, but the qualities that existed within the Waffen-SS in general, a contempt for death and a hatred for the enemy, can also be seen.

LEFT: A Waffen-SS machine-gun team reload their weapon, an MG34, during the drive to the English Channel in May 1940. Note how the loader is careful to keep his silhouette low so as not to present a target to the enemy. Throughout the long and bitter winter of 1939-40 the Waffen-SS had trained for the attack in the West. Hitler had told the men of the *Leibstandarte* they would soon be fighting in regions on which their fathers' blood had been shed. But the war fought in 1940 would be one of lightning strikes and manoeuvre, not the deadlock of trench warfare.

BELOW: Rivers are one of the main natural obstacles in warfare, and so in its training the Waffen-SS paid particular attention to overcoming such obstacles. The building of pontoon and temporary bridges, as well as the use of inflatable dinghies, was extensively practised. Thus, when the code word 'Danzig' was issued, signalling the beginning of the German attack in the West on 10 May, the *Leibstandarte* stormed across the Dutch border and raced on to Zarolle, where the Dutch had destroyed the bridge over the River Yssel. However, the Waffen-SS built improvised rafts to allow them to continue the advance into Holland.

RIGHT: A grim-faced Waffen-SS motorcyclist pauses during Army Group B's drive through the Low Countries in May 1940. He is wearing the distinctive SS camouflage smock, an item of clothing at first derided by the German Army. It is likely that he belongs to a divisional reconnaissance battalion. Such units were heavily armed and were used well in advance of the main body to collect tactical intelligence. The speed of the German advance in the 1940 campaign often resulted in vehicle bottlenecks among motorised units, which seems to have happened here, hence the sour expression on his face.

LEFT: Dunkirk after its evacuation by members of the British Expeditionary Force (BEF) and its capture by the Germans (note the German flag flying from the church tower). In the foreground can be seen the burnt-out remains of a BEF vehicle hit by German artillery fire. For the attack on Dunkirk the *Leibstandarte* had been attached to the 1st Panzer Division, and had already earned itself a place in the annals of German military history. During the drive through Holland, SS-Obersturmführer Hugo Kraas had led an assault group across the River Yssel and lanced some 64km (40 miles) into enemy territory, capturing 100 Dutch soldiers. For this action he was awarded the Iron Cross First Class, the first German soldier to receive such a decoration in the Western Campaign, receiving it on 25 May. By this time Hitler's bodyguard was at the Aá Canal and poised for the attack on Dunkirk itself, when news arrived of Hitler's 'halt order'. However, Dietrich's men were coming under accurate and concentrated enemy artillery fire, and so he decided to ignore the order and order a crossing. His men forced a crossing and stormed the heights overlooking the canal. Dietrich got away with disobeying orders.

RIGHT: The streets of Dunkirk after its capture by the Germans, early June 1940. Hitler's odd 'halt order', which prevented his armoured units attacking the boxed-in Allies in Flanders, was apparently motivated by Göring's wish that the Luftwaffe be allowed to deliver the fatal blow against the Allies at Dunkirk and thus share in the glory. That said, Hitler was also concerned that the French might somehow mount a counterattack from the south. The battle to hold the perimeter at Dunkirk had been fierce, and the *Leibstandarte* had found the resistance put up by the British Gloucestershire Regiment to be particularly strong. Indeed, the British resistance at Esquelberg was the most severe opposition the Waffen-SS encountered.

RIGHT: In attempting to stem the German advance, the Allies blew up strategically important bridges and mined vital roads. Here, Waffen-SS soldiers inspect the damage done by a land mine which has halted their vehicle. During the campaign in the West the German Army was once again critical of Waffen-SS recklessness. One officer of the *Deutschland* Regiment, for instance, wishing to set a good example, refused to yield to a British tank and fought standing with hand grenades until he was crushed beneath the tracks.

BELOW: For a second time in 25 years France suffered the devastation of war at the hands of the Germans, whose troops are seen here passing through a town in northern France, now reduced to rubble by aerial and artillery bombardment. By the end of May the three main fighting units of the Waffen-SS, the *Leibstandarte*, SS-Verfügungsdivision and the *Totenkopf* Division had been committed to the campaign. All three experienced heavy fighting, and in one particular incident near Cambrai, Eicke's men had suffered losses at the hands of British Matilda tanks, which proved impervious to the SS's 3.7cm guns.

HITLER'S BODYGUARD AT WAR

As in Poland, *Leibstandarte* fought well in the West in 1940, its performance earning its commander, 'Sepp' Dietrich, a Knight's Cross, Germany's highest gallantry award.

RIGHT: Soldiers of the *Leibstandarte* undertaking 'cook house' duties on the Western Front in June 1940. As can be seen, morale in the unit at this time is very high.

ABOVE: A bedraggled *Leibstandarte* soldier with two of his more smartly dressed officers. The men respected their officers, as illustrated by the frenzied attempts to rescue Dietrich when he was pinned down by British fire on 28 May 1940.

LEFT: One of the *Leibstandarte*'s 3.7cm anti-tank guns scores a direct hit on a BEF light tank in May 1940. At Wormhoudt Dietrich's men fought a savage battle with elements of the British 48th Division. The SS soldiers eventually secured the village, and then repulsed a number of British counterattacks, but in the process lost 23 killed and many more wounded. One officer, SS-Oberführer Mohnke, had some British prisoners executed after the battle had ended. He was never tried for this crime.

LEFT: Time for repairs during the advance into southern France. Following the fall of Dunkirk, the *Leibstandarte* struck for the River Aisne, encountering only token resistance from the French 11th Division. The race was on for the Marne, which the 2nd Battalion crossed on 12 June near St Avige. That evening the men of Hitler's bodyguard were told that Paris had fallen to the Germans – victory in the West was but days away.

RIGHT: A *Leibstandarte* officer asks for directions from a Belgian policeman in May 1940. In general the armies of both Belgium and Holland were in a poor state prior to the campaign, and were particularly deficient in anti-tank and anti-aircraft weapons. Their plan, therefore, was to delay the Germans as long as possible along river and canal lines, a strategy that singularly failed.

LEFT: Dietrich's men take a break during the pursuit of enemy forces during the Battle of France. In general the campaign against the French assumed the character of a pursuit, though the *Leibstandarte* still had to do some fighting. On 19 June, for example, as part of the 19th Panzer Division, it had to assault a French barricade on a bridge over the River Allier. The barricade was taken by a group commanded by SS-Obersturmführer Knittel, but then the bridge was blown up in the faces of the attackers.

ABOVE: An anti-tank crew push forward their 3.7cm anti-tank gun during the campaign in France. This weapon was found wanting by the Waffen-SS in 1940, both by the *Totenkopf* Division, as mentioned above, and by the *Leibstandarte*. When the latter attacked St Etienne on 22 June, the shells from its 3.7cm guns bounced off the hulls of attacking French tanks.

RIGHT: One of the *Totenkopf*'s trucks in France. Though the Waffen-SS had acquitted itself well during the campaign, the performance of the *Totenkopf* itself had left a lot to be desired. Though not lacking in courage, it had suffered high losses due to the spirit of recklessness that existed within its ranks. At the end of May alone, for example, the division had suffered 1140 casualties in a 10-day period, and the loss of 300 officers was particularly serious. The loss of equipment during this period had also been heavy: 46 trucks, eight armoured cars and an unspecified amount of mortars, heavy machine guns and rifles. Himmler was not amused.

ABOVE: Troops of the *Totenkopf* Division during the campaign in the West, 1940. The relationship between Eicke's men and their army counterparts took a turn for the worse during the SS men's journey to the front. There were large traffic jams in the rear of Army Group B as the *Totenkopf* Division moved out of the reserve, and Eicke and his men traded insults and argued with army commanders and their men regarding the right of way as they headed for the front.

RIGHT: An unusual photograph taken towards the end of the Battle of France, which shows a mule train being driven by what appears to be Moroccan drivers supplying the German Army in the field. The colonial troops are presumably captured French Army personnel. These Moroccans are the lucky ones, for those who were captured by the Waffen-SS, such as those captured by the *Totenkopf* Division on 19 May near Cambrai, were usually summarily shot.

BELOW: Two members of the *Totenkopf* Division during an attack on a fortified position in France. The man on the right is armed with a Mauser 7.63mm machine pistol fitted with a detachable stock. German military manuals slated this weapon, 'because the high power of its cartridge, its low weight its recoil and high cyclic rate of fire make it of little use for ordinary military purposes. Used as a pistol this weapon functions so rapidly that it is impossible to distinguish between cartridges as they explode. Regardless of the strength of the firer, the recoil forces the weapon upwards and backwards. It is impossible to hold down even with both hands'. Despite this, in Waffen-SS circles it was considered a useful weapon 'against mobs'.

CHAPTER SEVEN

Balkan Interlude

The Waffen-SS in Yugoslavia and Greece

Hitler did not want a conflict in the Balkans, and had restrained his Axis partner Mussolini on several occasions during the spring and summer of 1940 from initiating plans for an Italian invasion of Yugoslavia and Greece. Mussolini, jealous of German successes, reluctantly accepted Hitler's wishes, as he was dependent on Germany for raw materials. In May 1940, Mussolini's frustration was further heightened when the German armies drove the British forces off the continent and brought France to her knees; it now seemed certain that Germany would win the war.

LEFT: The Waffen-SS invades Yugoslavia, April 1941.

OPPOSITE: SS-Gruppenführer 'Sepp' Dietrich, commander of the *Leibstandarte*, photographed during the campaign in Greece, in which Hitler's bodyguard played an important part in securing a German victory.

DISASTER FOR ITALIAN ARMS

Determined to win his own war, on the morning of 28 October 1940 Mussolini invaded Greece from Albania. He proclaimed the birth of a 'New Roman Empire' that was to recreate the glories of ancient Rome. However, a month later the Greeks expelled the Italians from their country, and had occupied a quarter of Albania by the middle of January 1941.

Mussolini's 'Greek disaster' had engendered a fundamental change in the relationship between him and Hitler. The latter made no attempt to conceal his displeasure at the 'Italian adventure', which had jeopardised the Axis position in southeastern Europe.

In November 1940, as part of his ambition to control the Balkans, plans for a more effective invasion of Greece had been formulated by Hitler, codenamed 'Operation Marita'. It required the deployment of 16 divisions in bases in southern Romania, from where they would drive south into Greece. The initial idea was to seize the Greek mainland north of the Aegean sea, but with the landing of British troops in Greece in early March, the plan was refined. Hitler now decided to occupy the whole peninsula and the island of Crete.

The Tripartite Pact formed between Rome-Berlin-Tokyo was the cornerstone of the Axis. Another nation that joined was Yugoslavia, on 25 March 1941, albeit under intense German diplomatic pressure. The route to the Greek border seemed assured. However, the Yugoslavs overthrew their pro-Nazi government. The young Peter II was proclaimed king and a new anti-German government established. This was a problem for Hitler, for a hostile Yugoslav government was a potential threat to both operations 'Marita' and 'Barbarossa' (the planned German invasion of Russia).

THE INVASION OF YUGOSLAVIA

Therefore, Hitler ordered that 'Operation Marita' be expanded to include an invasion of Yugoslavia, ordering that the blow be carried out with total ruthlessness. Operation 'Marita' would be launched simultaneously with the invasion of Yugoslavia, while Operation 'Barbarossa' was to be postponed for 'up to four weeks'.

In early February 1942 the *Leibstandarte* was transfered to Romania in preparation for 'Marita'. An order to continue with all haste to Temesvar in southwestern Romania was given to the SS-Verfügungsdivision (now renamed the *Das Reich* Division) on 28 March. The division's entire strength was relocated to its new quarters in less than a week – a remarkable achievement.

Operation 'Marita' opened on 6 April 1941. As part of XLI Panzer Corps, under the command of General Georg-Hans

LEFT: German troops in Greece in April 1941. Hitler's Blitzkrieg in the Balkans secured another easy German victory, but had delayed the invasion of the Soviet Union. For Himmler and the Waffen-SS, the war in Russia was to be the real test of strength, not some insignificant side-show in southern Europe.

The conquest of Greece could now begin. The 12th Army, led by General Wilhelm List, composed of four panzer divisions, eight infantry divisions, the élite *Grossdeutschland* Regiment and the *Leibstandarte*, was ready to thrust into Greece on 6 April. The *Leibstandarte* attacked from Romania, through Bulgaria, southern Yugoslavia and onto Greek soil.

THE *LEIBSTANDARTE* IN GREECE

Skopje was taken in the course of its advance, and within three days it had taken the stronghold of Monastir on the Yugoslav-Greek border. The *Leibstandare* then stormed the vital Klidi Pass, the gateway to Greece, then the Klissura Pass after heavy fighting.

The *Leibstandarte*'s next objective was Koritza, the headquarters of III Greek Corps. The approaches to Kastoria were being reconnoitred when concentrated Greek artillery fire made the SS troops withdraw. It soon became clear that infantry alone could not take these positions, so it was necessary to call on the *Leibstandarte*'s regimental artillery, backed up by a squadron of Stuka dive-bombers. A furious aerial and artillery bombardment was unleashed on the hapless Greeks.

Before their occupants had time to recover, the Greek positions were overcome. SS-Sturmbannführer Kurt Meyer's armoured cars approached Kastoria at breakneck speed and encountered large columns of retreating Greek troops, who were so shocked that they quickly surrendered. By late afternoon Kastoria was in German hands.

On 19 April, the *Leibstandarte* was ordered southwest to capture the Metsovan Pass, which was achieved the following day. Some sixteen Greek Army divisions were now isolated to the west of the Pindus range and forced to surrender on 21 April. SS-Gruppenführer 'Sepp' Dietrich accepted the Greek surrender, an act which infuriated Mussolini, who insisted on his share of the military glory. Formal surrender

Reinhardt, the *Das Reich* Division was involved in the thrust on Belgrade. General Reinhardt had promised movement priority as a prize to the first unit to the initial objective: the main road leading from Alibunar to Zagreb. It seemed to SS-Gruppenführer Paul 'Papa' Hausser there would be little chance of his unit achieving this prize, as *Das Reich* had to traverse boggy marshland. However, he still believed his troops would reach Belgrade first.

The push by Das Reich began at 0900 hours on 11 April. Its newly formed Motorcycle Reconnaissance Battalion rode along railway tracks and reached the road first. When the rest of the division arrived, it received orders from corps that all units were to halt on the river bank, the retreating Yugoslavs were not to be pursued over the Danube.

DAS REICH TAKES BELGRADE

On 11 April, after a nightmare journey, SS-Hauptsturmführer Fritz Klingenberg and his motorcycle reconnaissance troops reached the Danube first. However, it was so swollen by floodwater that none of the bridges remained intact; a crossing seemed impossible. Disregarding the halt order, Klingenberg decided to investigate the opposite bank. A captured old fishing boat enabled him to ferry himself, 10 volunteers and their motorcycles onto the opposite side. This minuscule force set forth and reached Belgrade. By sheer bluff he persuaded the city's mayor to surrender the city, and on Easter Day the German authorities took over the capital. The war in Yugoslavia was all but over, and so the *Das Reich* Division returned to Temesvar in Romania, and then on to Austria to undertake training. On 14 May, Klingenberg was decorated with the Knight's Cross for his bold victory by a delighted Hitler.

ceremonies were therefore organised, where Italian interests were fully represented.

The British Expeditionary Force was now alone in Greece and had its back against the wall. On 24 April the *Leibstandarte*, in pursuit of the retreating forces, moved eastwards towards Navpaktos on the Gulf of Corinth. The chase continued across the gulf and on through Peloponnesus, as most of the British troops had managed to evacuate over the gulf to Patras, protected by gallant rearguard actions.

ANOTHER EASY VICTORY

Meyer lost radio contact with the regiment and was unable to obtain new orders. He gambled on sending a patrol in two boats across the gulf to investigate. An agonising 90-minute wait ensued before the two boats reappeared, with 40 British prisoners! Meyer then commandeered every fishing boat available and ferried the rest of his battalion across into Patras. Meyer gave orders to the 2nd Company of his battalion to make contact with the units of Paratroop Regiment 2. He despatched them east to Corinth with orders to commandeer whatever vehicles were available locally, as no heavy transport had kept up with the advance. The SS men returned to Patras, and then began their march south towards Olympia in pursuit of the fleeing British. However, the Greek Army's total collapse and the successful evacuation of most of the British and Commonwealth forces rendered any further advance unnecessary.

On 27 April 1941 German troops entered Athens, and three days later they were in complete control of the country. The *Leibstandarte* was accorded the honour of participating in the victory parade in Athens.

Though the campaign in the Balkans had been a brilliant example of Blitzkrieg war, for the Waffen-SS, and the German armed forces as a whole, it was a distraction. The real test lay ahead: the war against the Soviet Union. For the Waffen-SS this was to be an ideological campaign, in which the standard rules of war were to be put aside in what Himmler's ideologically motivated soldiers came to regard as a holy war, a crusade against Bolshevism and the 'sub-humanity' who lived in the Soviet Union. A war of brutality was about to begin.

BELOW: The swastika is raised over Athens on 27 April 1941. The Germans were in complete control of Greece three days later, having bagged a total of 223,000 Greek and 21,900 British prisoners. German losses for the entire Balkan campaign were 2559 dead and 5820 wounded.

ABOVE: The invasion of Yugoslavia gets under way. The *Das Reich* Division had performed a remarkable feat of logistics on the eve of the Balkan war, moving its entire strength from Vesoul in eastern France to Temesvar in southwestern Romania in less than a week. However, there occurred a number of clashes between army and Waffen-SS personnel. In one instance, an SS officer became so incensed when an army column tried to pass his unit that he halted the army vehicles and shouted at its commander: 'If you drive on without my permission, I will order my men to open fire on your column. This and other incidents, including an SS officer placing mines under the wheels of an army truck, prompted the Commander-in-Chief of the German Army, Field Marshal von Brauchitsch, to complain formerly to Himmler.

RIGHT: Soldiers of the *Das Reich* Division during the campaign in Yugoslavia. The division began its campaign at 0900 hours on 11 April 1941. It soon became clear that the poorly equipped Yugoslav Army would be no match for the Germans; indeed, the main enemy was the weather, as rain turned roads into quagmires, making rapid movement all but impossible as *Das Reich*'s vehicles sank into the mud.

LEFT: German motorcycle troops escort a column of Leichter Panzerspahwagen (Sd Kfz) 221 armoured cars during Operation 'Marita'. The conquest of the Balkans was the responsibility of Field Marshal Wilhelm List's 12th Army The Waffen-SS component was minuscule, but the high-profile capture of Belgrade by the *Das Reich* Division, ahead of the army's élite *Grossdeutschland* Regiment, was a feather in the cap for both Himmler and SS-Gruppenführer Paul Hausser, the *Das Reich* Division's commander.

BELOW: Stuck in the mud during the advance to Belgrade. The race to the Yugoslav capital was won by SS-Hauptsturmführer Fritz Klingenberg of the *Das Reich*'s Motorcycle Reconnaissance Battalion. He and 10 of his men reached Belgrade on 11 April 1941, and upon entering found its streets deserted. Reaching the German Embassy, Klingenberg and the German Military Attaché decided to try to take the city by bluff. Finding the mayor, Klingenberg announced he was the commander of a major assault force positioned just outside the city, and that if he did not receive the city's immediate surrender he would order a massive air strike by Stuka dive-bombers. The terrified mayor handed Belgrade over to Klingenberg and his 10 men.

RIGHT: 'Sepp' Dietrich during the *Leibstandarte*'s spectacular campaign in Greece. The first success his men enjoyed was at the Klidi Pass, the gateway to Greece. Heavily defended by Australians and New Zealanders, it took two days of fighting before it had been secured, during the course of which the SS repulsed tanks.

LEFT: German troops and armour on patrol in the Balkans some time after the area had been conquered by the Third Reich. The fighting in the Balkans provides an insight into the fighting spirit of Waffen-SS soldiers. During the *Leibstandarte*'s seizure of the Klissura Pass on 11 April, SS-Sturmbannführer Kurt Meyer and his men were pinned down. 'How can I get [my men] to take the first leap? In my distress I feel the smooth roundness of an egg hand grenade in my hand. I shout at the group. Everybody looks thunderstruck at me as I brandish the hand grenade, pull the pin, and roll it precisely behind the last man. Never again did I witness such a concerted leap forward as at that second. As if bitten by tarantulas, we dive around the rock spur and into a fresh crater. The spell is broken. The grenade has cured our lameness.'

RIGHT: The new overlords in the Balkans. For Himmler's soldiers the campaign in southern Europe had almost been too easy: the *Leibstandarte* had cut through Greek and Commonwealth forces like a hot knife through butter, taking Kastoria and the Metsovon Pass and forcing the surrender of 16 enemy divisions within the space of a week. Dietrich accepted the surrender personally, which offended Mussolini, who wanted Italy to be accorded a share of the glory.

BELOW: As soon as the campaign in the Balkans was over the Waffen-SS pulled out to prepare for the invasion of the Soviet Union. Though the Blitzkrieg had once again carried all before it, Operation 'Barbarossa', the German attack on the Soviet Union, had been postponed, thereby denying the Germans around half of the best campaigning season in Russia. Nevertheless, morale among both army and Waffen-SS units was high, and the war in Russia was looked upon with relish.

CHAPTER EIGHT

'Barbarossa'

The invasion of the Soviet Union, 1941

The Waffen-SS, the Third Reich's ideological military élite, was to encounter a new kind of war in Russia, one based on a clash of political creeds. To Himmler and his officers it took the form of a Wagnerian struggle of the Herrenvolk (master race) against the Untermenschen (sub-humans). Its aim was to create a vast area in the East which could be populated by a Germanic Nordic race, and to deal with those groups the Nazi Party despised most: the Jews, Slavs and Bolsheviks.

The Soviet Red Army had been decimated by Stalin's purges in the 1930s, when he carried out the systematic destruction of the Soviet High command, the primary motive being to secure his position as absolute ruler of the Soviet Union. Some 35,000 officers were either dismissed, imprisoned or executed, and in 1941 the Red Army was still suffering from the loss of some of its ablest officers. Thus on the eve of Operation 'Barbarossa', the German invasion of the Soviet Union, though the Red Army fielded 230 divisions totalling some 12 million men supported by 20,000 tanks and 8000 aircraft against three million German soldiers accompanied by 3330 tanks and 2770 aircraft, many Soviet units were poorly led and motivated.

WAFFEN-SS DISPOSITIONS FOR 'BARBAROSSA'

Waffen-SS units were deployed among the various army commands. Field Marshal Gerd von Rundstedt's Army Group South contained the *Leibstandarte* and *Wiking* Divisions. The *Das Reich* Division was allotted to General Heinz Guderian's 2nd Panzer Group, which formed part of Army Group Centre commanded by Field Marshal Fedor von Bock. The weakest of the army groups, Army Group North, was commanded by Field Marshal Ritter von Leeb and contained

LEFT: Himmler in triumphant mood during the early phase of 'Barbarossa'. The Germans are experiencing success all along the front, and his divisions are winning fresh laurels against the 'eternal enemy of Germany'.

OPPOSITE: Jubilant members of *Das Reich* in June 1941.

Eicke's *Totenkopf* Division, which was a part of General Erich Höpner's 4th Panzer Group. The *Polizei* Division was part of Army Group North's reserves, while SS-Kampfgruppe (Battle Group) *Nord* and SS Infantry Regiment 9 were deployed as part of the Norway Mountain Corps under the command of Colonel-General von Falkenhorst. These two units were committed to the far northern sector of the front in Finland.

GERMAN OBJECTIVES

Army Group South had the initial task of cutting off all Soviet armies west of the Dnieper, capturing Kiev, Kharkov and the Crimea, then pushing on to the River Volga and to the Caucasian oil fields. This over-ambitious plan involved 46 divisions. The 1st Panzer Group had the objective of breaking through the Russian lines south of Kowel and cutting off Red Army units to the southwest. The *Leibstandarte* Division was assigned to XIV Corps of the 1st Panzer Group, and was expected to make an initial advance of 480km (300 miles) over compacted dirt roads. Opposing Army Group Centre were the natural defence lines of the Rivers Pruth, San, Bug and Dnieper, around which were deployed 69 infantry, 11 cavalry and 28 armoured Russian divisions.

The greatest continuous land battle in history erupted at 0315 hours on 22 June 1941. Within days all the Waffen-SS formations except the *Polizei* Division were in action, with

ABOVE: A Waffen-SS armoured car column races over a deserted Russian bridge after Soviet border positions were smashed by the 4th Panzer group on the first day of Operation 'Barbarossa', 22 June 1941. Höpner's troops encountered only light resistance, and on the first day alone advanced 80km (50 miles).

two brigades of Himmler's Kommandostab RFSS, SS Infantry Brigade 1 and the SS cavalry brigade being deployed immediately behind the front to deal with bypassed enemy units.

On 27 June the *Leibstandarte* Division was committed, and went into combat on 1 July when it crossed the River Vistula southwest of Zamosc. Because the 1st Panzer Group's pincer movement had cut deep into Soviet territory, General von Mackensen's III Panzer Corps was cut off near Rovno. The *Leibstandarte* was ordered to re-establish contact with it. Soon Waffen-SS forward elements were engaging Soviet tanks; these were dealt with and Klevan was taken. To the east of the town the *Leibstandarte*'s reconnaissance battalion discovered an empty, blood-soaked ambulance beside an abandoned German howitzer. Nearby lay the corpses of several German soldiers, their bodies mutilated. 'Sepp' Dietrich, the *Leibstandarte*'s commander, ordered that the Russians 'must be slaughtered ruthlessly' – the war of atrocity had begun.

Zhitomir and Kiev became the next objective of the 1st Panzer Group, with the *Leibstandarte* providing flank cover.

It had to fight off frenzied Russian attacks, often supported by armour, but it maintained its discipline and on 7 July its spearhead units breached the Stalin Line defences at Mirupol. Against stiff resistance it pushed eastwards towards Zhitomir, but heavy rain rendered many of the roads unpassable, forcing Hitler's bodyguard to go across country. That night the *Leibstandarte* Division was at Romanovka. The next day the vital Keednov road junction was captured by the *Leibstandarte* in a battle principally fought by SS-Obersturmbannführer Kurt Meyer's reconnaissance battalion. His troops, supported by 8.8cm artillery fire, stormed across the River Teterev.

The German Armed Forces High Command (OKW) believed Army Group South had achieved its primary objective and destroyed the bulk of the Soviet armies in the southwest. The troops at the front, however, did not share this optimism, a view backed up by a Soviet counteroffensive aimed at cutting the main German supply route, the Rollbahn. The attacks were finally repulsed, though only after ferocious hand-to-hand combat, with heavy casualties on both sides. The *Leibstandarte* captured Shepkova on 9 July, allowing it to go onto the offensive. But on 10 July Hitler unexpectedly altered the attack in the south, ordering a drive towards Uman. The subsequent fighting around the Uman Pocket earned special praise for the *Leibstandarte*'s contribution from General Kempf: 'Today, with the battle of annihilation around Uman concluded, I wish to recognise, and express my special gratitude to the *Leibstandarte SS Adolf Hitler* for its exemplary efforts and incomparable bravery.'

WIKING'S WAR

The *Wiking* Division, led by the *Westland* Regiment, deployed on 29 June 1941 and advanced through Soviet-occupied Poland. At Lemberg, the Soviet 32nd Infantry Division was encountered by its spearhead units the next day. The Waffen-SS soldiers had to endure considerable pressure before the arrival of the division's reconnaissance battalion's tanks finally swung the balance in the Germans favour. *Wiking* then forced a crossing of the River Slucz and, with other Waffen-SS troops, was soon engaged in heavy fighting in this area, which was part of the Stalin Line defences. The fighting raged back and forth until the Army's 1st Mountain Division arrived and relieved the beleaguered Waffen-SS.

Meanwhile, the *Leibstandarte* advanced to Zaselye, where it ran into a furious Russian counterattack. Holding on grimly, the *Leibstandarte* held its ground for a week against determined Russian attempts to eject it. The Soviet attacks finally ceased on 17 August, allowing the *Leibstandarte* to resume the advance. The next objective was Cherson, which fell to the SS after three days of fierce fighting.

As the Germans pushed deeper into the Soviet Union, Hitler changed his plans once again. Large numbers of Soviet troops had been withdrawing into the Crimea, and he was determined to eradicate this potential threat to the flank of the German advance. The *Leibstandarte* took part in the securing of the Crimea, and then continued eastwards towards Rostov.

In northern Russia, General Erich Höpner's 4th Panzer Group drove towards Leningrad. Its principal units were XXXXI and LVI Panzer Corps, with the 269th Infantry and *Totenkopf* Divisions in reserve and General Busch's 16th Army providing flank protection.

On 22 June 1941, the 4th Panzer Group smashed through Soviet border positions and headed towards the key bridges over the River Dvina. Höpner's troops encountered extremely light resistance, and were able to cover 80km (50 miles) on the first day; by 26 June they were 320km (200 miles) into Soviet-held territory and had captured the bridges.

THE BLOODY ADVANCE TO LENINGRAD

A considerable gap had appeared between the southern flank of General von Manstein's LVI Panzer Corps and the northern flank of the 16th Army. The *Totenkopf* Division was used to plug the gap, and by the end of June was fighting off fanatical Russian assaults. Eicke himself was wounded during this period, but his division had reached the dark forests and swamps to the west of Lake Ilmen by 21 July. The Soviets had withdrawn to the Luga Line that ran along the Mshaga and Luga rivers. But the Russians continued to offer dogged resistance, the Soviet 34th Army smashing into the German flanks. In response the 3rd Motorised Division and the

Totenkopf Division combined to launch a counterattack. The subsequent fighting destroyed eight Soviet divisions.

On 22 August, the *Totenkopf* Division pressed on towards the Rivers Lovat and Pola, where Russian troops were dug in in strong positions. Attempts to force a crossing failed, and Red Army counterattacks were so powerful that the Germans were forced to withdraw. The *Totenkopf* managed to resume the advance, but the division had been weakened considerably. Thus when LVI Panzer Corps demanded it cross the River Pola on 30 August, its temporary commander, SS-Brigadeführer und Generalmajor der Waffen-SS Georg Keppler, appealed to von Manstein, who agreed the attack should be postponed for a few days (though Soviet attacks meant Keppler's men had no respite). On 5 September the weather briefly improved, allowing the *Totenkopf* Division, supported by the 503 Infantry Regiment, to throw itself over the Pola. However, the rains had returned again and furious counterattacks once more were being mounted by the Red Army. Russian booby traps and mines inflicted many casualties and slowed the *Totenkopf*'s progress. By 12 September the division was once more on the defensive, fighting off determined Russian counterattacks.

As autumn gave way to winter, it became clear that 'Barbarossa' would not defeat the Red Army in 1941. The Germans had achieved spectacular victories, had destroyed thousands of enemy aircraft and vehicles, as well as capturing hundreds of thousands of prisoners. The soldiers of the Waffen-SS had once again showed themselves to be fanatical soldiers, and had on more than one occasion saved the day when Russian units had launched counterattacks. But the Waffen-SS, like the German Army as a whole, had suffered massive losses, in both men and war material. The *Deutschland* and *Der Führer* Regiments, for example, had each been forced to disband one battalion and redistribute the men. And now, as the weather deteriorated in Russia, the Waffen-SS prepared to fight another campaign against the hated Bolshevik enemy. But first Himmler's men had to get through the Russian winter.

LEFT: Soldiers of the *Totenkopf* Division during the early stages of the Russian Campaign. The man on the right has a 9mm Steyr-Solothurn machine pistol. This weapon was widely used by both the SS and police, being part of the war stocks seized from Austria in 1938.

LEFT: A Waffen-SS officer addresses his unit immediately prior to the attack on Russia. On his sleeve he wears a German Army eagle rather than one in the SS style. Many Waffen-SS officers at this time wore army designs, the probable reason being the shortage of the relevant insignia. Another possibility is that those officers who transferred from the army wished to retain a link with their past. The soldiers of the Waffen-SS were constantly reminded that the war in Russia was an ideological crusade, and as they were the living embodiment of the National Socialist doctrine of the superiority of Nordic blood, they were expected to show no mercy towards the 'sub-human' enemy, who stood in the way of Germany's colonisation of the East. Himmler stated: 'I believe the business we have out there is so exalted, so great, so unique and many sided ... I propose that we be pitiless in the settlement policy because these new provinces must become Germanic, blond provinces of Germany – must become National Socialist provinces ... The new provinces must really be a Germanic blood-wall, must be a wall within which there is no blood-question, no children-question, but where one day that question will again take precedence and we will become a Volk of abundant children.' The war in Russia was to finally settle the conflict between two opposing political systems.

RIGHT: Smiling faces of the *Leibstandarte* prior to the invasion of Russia. The Germans expected that Russia would be crushed quickly by the Blitzkrieg, as Hitler stated in his directive on 18 December 1940: 'The German armed forces must be prepared, even before the conclusion of the war against England, to crush Soviet Russia in a rapid campaign.' Though the campaign in the Balkans had postponed 'Barbarossa', the new date – 22 June – must have appealed to Hitler's sense of destiny. It was, after all, the first anniversary of the signing of the armistice with France the year before, and within a day of the anniversary of Napoleon's crossing of the River Niemen into Russia with his *Grande Armée* in 1812. For the attack he mustered 11 armies, four of them panzer, and three air fleets, totalling around three million men. They were divided among three army groups – North, Centre and South – the objective of which were Leningrad in the north and the Ukraine (Moscow was to be taken afterwards). The Red Army was to be annihilated in huge battles of encirclement in the Baltic states, Belorussia and the Ukraine to prevent its escape into the interior of the Soviet Union. An operation of this magnitude had never been undertaken before, and as Hitler excitedly stated: 'When the attack on Russia starts the world will hold its breath.'

RIGHT: Two men of the *Totenkopf* Division chat with a Russian civilian during the early stages of 'Barbarossa'. At first many Russians saw the Germans as their liberators, such was the hatred for the government in Moscow among many areas of the Soviet Union. The idea that a massive partisan movement sprang up the moment the Germans invaded Russia is a myth. However, the ideological nature of the war, which led to German units committing atrocities against civilians, and the actions of the Einsatzgruppen (SS Special Action Groups) that followed the armies, rounding up and shooting Jews and other 'undesirables', quickly alienated large sections of the population, forcing the Germans to deploy troops in rear areas against partisans.

LEFT: As the Germans penetrated into Russia they erased as much of the communist culture as possible. Here, a Waffen-SS soldier is destroying a statue of Lenin. Such acts were symbolic of the SS's desire to remove all vestiges of Bolshevism from the face of the earth. That included its supporters as well, as Himmler was to tell his senior commanders: 'This 200 million Russian Volk must be militarily and humanly annihilated and bled to death.' It is a tragic irony that thousands of Jews who had escaped the Nazis during the conquest of Poland now found themselves trapped by the German advance.

BELOW: Columns of smoke pour into the sky from burning buildings and Russian tanks following an engagement with German panzers in late June 1941. At the beginning of the Russian Campaign the strength of the Waffen-SS was as follows: *Leibstandarte* Division (10,796), *Wiking* Division (19,377), *Totenkopf* Division (18,754), *Nord* Division (10,573), *Das Reich* Division (19,021), *Polizei* Division (17,347), Kommandostab Reichsführer-SS (18,438), Administrative Department (4007), reserve units (29,809), Inspectorate of Concentration Camps (7200), SS guard battalions (2159), SS garrison posts (992), SS officer and NCO schools (1028), and SS Volunteer Battalion *Nordost* (904). The latter unit was made up of Finns who had volunteered for service in the Waffen-SS. Within days most of the Waffen-SS divisions were in action against the Russians in the so-called 'battle of the frontiers'. In this engagement the Red Army was decisively beaten. General Alfred Philippi was a Wehrmacht officer who fought in these battles and describes them thus: 'The Soviets fought in separate, uncoordinated groups, apparently without unified leadership; obstinate resistance alternated with withdrawal Some Red Army units disappeared into the vast forests, only to turn up again in the rear of the advancing German troops. The result was a series of local engagements, carried out by day and night, with severe losses to both side. Again and again portions of the Russian forces succeeded in breaking out eastwards, at points where the gaps in the net drawn around them were widest. There was no question of surrender. Nevertheless, the general view was that such tactics would be unable to prevent the planned encirclement and the elimination of the Soviet forces.' At first easy progress was made in the north and centre, though Rundstedt's Army Group South encountered desperate resistance. By the end of June the Germans had taken Brest Litovsk and encircled Russian forces in pockets at Bialystok, Novogrudok and Volkovysk. But greater victories were to follow: Army Group Centre captured Vitebsk on 9 July; six days later a breakthrough in the centre led to the encirclement and fall of Smolensk, cutting off a Soviet concentration of 300,000 men between Orsha and Smolensk. The *Das Reich* Division was part of Army Group Centre, and soon encountered one of the many problems associated with campaigning in Russia: the Waffen-SS, and German Army, was designed for mobile warfare on good roads backed up by extensive rail systems. But in Russia there were few all-weather roads and even fewer main railway lines. The division's vehicles were thus forced to move across country, and when they neared the Pripet Marshes the sandy soil slowed the advance and ruined engines. In addition, though the average Waffen-SS soldier had been taught to hate the Soviet Union, he knew little about the individual Russian soldier or civilian, and even less about the terrain he would be fighting over for the next four years.

ABOVE: Members of the 4th SS Division *SS-Polizei* take a welcome break from the fighting in Russia. This division did not take part in the initial moves of Operation 'Barbarossa', but by August 1941 had been fully committed to the fighting. The scorching heat and choking dust of the Russian summer sapped the energy of the troops. Nevertheless, the victories continued: at the end of July the *Leibstandarte* Division had participated in the reduction of the Uman Pocket, which netted over 100,000 men from the Russian 6th and 12th Armies. Special praise was reserved for the *Leibstandarte* during this action.

RIGHT: A Panzer III speeds over a pontoon bridge erected by SS pioneers. Hitler's panzers made such rapid progress during 'Barbarossa' that dangerously wide gaps started to appear between German formations. The flanks of III Panzer Corps, for example, were attacked by Red Army units operating from the Pripet Marshes. The *Leibstandarte* was therefore ordered to provide flank protection. Soon the Waffen-SS soldiers were fighting off savage Soviet attacks, often supported by armour.

ABOVE: Waffen-SS pioneers inspect a bridge destroyed by the Russians as they retreated as part of their 'scorched earth' policy, an effort to deprive the invaders of supplies and transport facilities as they penetrated ever deeper into the Soviet Union. The Russians believed that such tactics would delay the German onslaught, but in the case of bridges the Germans simply installed temporary bridges in a matter of

hours. The speed of the German advance greatly surprised the Russians. During the sealing off of Red Army units at Uman and Kiev, for example, victory was won not so much by direct assaults as by penetrations of such depths that the Russian strategists did not notice the closing trap until it was too late. And the motorised Waffen-SS divisions came into their own, covering vast distances and sweeping all before them.

LEFT: A Soviet supply column following an attack by Luftwaffe aircraft, probably Stukas. Attacks on Soviet airfields during the first stage of 'Barbarossa' were successful beyond the wildest German dreams. Hundreds of aircraft were destroyed on the ground, sitting out in the open in neat rows. Having achieved complete air superiority, the Luftwaffe concentrated its efforts against enemy troop concentrations, communications and supply columns. The scene shown here was repeated on dozens of occasions in June 1941.

ABOVE: When Hitler diverted Army Group South to envelop Uman on 10 July, the *Leibstandarte* Division was allocated to XXXVIII Corps. Savage fighting followed, but on 31 July Hitler's bodyguard was ordered to push towards Novo Archangelsk to close the Uman Pocket. In a desperate attempt to break out the Russians flung armour and infantry against the Waffen-SS soldiers. However, the SS held its lines and the Uman Pocket was sealed. Some of the 100,000 Red Army soldiers captured during this epic engagement are shown here.

BELOW: As one Red Army army after another was destroyed, the bag of Russian prisoners became so large that the Germans could not cope. These men, gathered at a railhead and guarded by SS and police personnel, are waiting to be transported west to 'internment camps'. A hastily constructed extermination camp for Russian officers was set up at Birkenau, which began operations in the autumn of 1941. It was part of the larger Auschwitz camp and its commandant was SS-Sturmbannführer Friedrich Hartjenstein.

ABOVE: A German machine-gun team surveys the scene across the vast Russian steppe. On the ground the Germans were often surprised by the ferocity of Russian resistance. On 27 June 1941, for example, the *Totenkopf* Division was in Lithuania and its reconnaissance battalion was forced to repel a series of fanatical Russian counterattacks. The Waffen-SS soldiers suffered no casualties but were shaken by the determination of their 'sub-human' foe.

RIGHT: Waffen-SS troops and armoured cars pour into Russia. As the fighting continued in Russia, the Waffen-SS began to react predictably to the continuing enemy resistance. Max Simon, a regimental commander in the *Totenkopf* Division, described bypassed groups of Russian soldiers as 'bandits', and ordered that they should be dealt with ruthlessly. Very soon units of the *Totenkopf* Division were shooting the majority of Russian stragglers they encountered, especially those who offered any sort of resistance.

RIGHT: A Waffen-SS officer awards the Iron Cross First Class to another officer in the field. He is the lucky one, for many of the medals won during Operation 'Barbarossa' were posthumous: 'Blood is the price of victory. Philanthropists may easily imagine that there is a skilful method of disarming and overcoming the enemy without great bloodshed, and that this is the proper tendency of the art of war. That is an error which must be extirpated.' (Karl von Clausewitz)

BELOW: Waffen-SS engineers undertake the task of clearing a road of mines. The contribution of engineer units during the early phases of the Russian Campaign cannot be overstated. Often operating under heavy fire and difficult conditions, they cleared roads of mines, built temporary bridges and undertook a plethora of other tasks. Their efforts allowed the infantry and armour to continue the advance, and though they did not win much glory they paid a high price in blood.

ABOVE: A Russian tank receives a direct hit. German tank crews swept aside all opposition during Operation 'Barbarossa', which in the main consisted of obsolete, thinly armoured vehicles such as the BT-5. There were rumours of a new Russian tank, heavier than the Panzer IV, but these were discarded. German tactics were also better. Heinz Guderian, Germany's panzer genius, committed tanks in 'mass, not driblets', but Russian tanks were used in ones and twos.

RIGHT: Knight's Cross at his neck (awarded for his single-handed capture of Belgrade during the Balkan Campaign immediately prior to 'Barbarossa', and awarded by Hitler himself), SS-Obersturmbannführer Fritz Klingenberg leads the motorcycle battalion of the *Das Reich* Division during the Russian Campaign. Klingenberg had volunteered for the SS-Verfügungstruppe in 1934, and after attending officer school at Bad Tölz in 1935 became a company commander in the *Germania* Regiment.

BELOW: Time to pause while enquiries as to the location of the enemy are made on the field telephone. As June gave way to July and then August, German casualties mounted. Waffen-SS units were caught up in almost continuous fighting. In late August, for example, the *Wiking* Division endeavoured to force a crossing of the River Dnieper at Dnepropetrovsk. Unfortunately a Russian artillery school was located at this spot, and its cadets expertly pinpointed the Waffen-SS units as they tried to cross. In the face of a frenzied artillery barrage the *Nordland*, *Westland* and *Germania* Regiments forced a crossing, the former pushing north towards Mogila Ostraya, while the other two reinforced the German units on the bridgehead's western edge. On 6-7 September they captured the heights at Kamenka. But then the Red Army launched a surprise counterattack that lanced some 32km (20 miles) into German-held territory, and so the *Leibstandarte* was hastily withdrawn back over the Dnieper to deal with this new threat. Following this short reversal, the bridgehead was established on the Dnieper and the *Leibstandarte* resumed its advance, moving across the Nogai steppe in the first week of September. One Waffen-SS grenadier recorded in his diary: 'There is very little water and what there is is salty. Coffee is salt flavoured, the soup is over-salted, but we are pleased even to get this tepid liquid for this is true desert country. Movement is visible for miles; clouds of choking, red brown dust hang over our moving columns and pinpoint our exact positions. Paradoxically, the only sign of life are the dead tree trunks of telegraph poles. Without them it would be difficult to orientate oneself. Sometimes we find a melon field and gorge, but the unripe ones have unhappy effects!' Next came the securing of the Crimea, which the *Leibstandarte* took part in by attempting to force the western edge of the Perekop isthmus. However, against deep minefields, well prepared fortifications and armoured trains it failed to effect a breach. Trying its luck on the eastern edge, the Waffen-SS soldiers at last broke through under cover of thick fog in a dawn attack. The Red Army fought well, but eventually Kleist's 1st Panzer Group, now renamed 1st Panzer Army, smashed through and raced towards Rostov with the intention of catching and destroying the enemy in a vast encircling movement. By early October the Russians had been broken, a grenadier in the *Leibstandarte* noting: 'We were in among them like Hussars cutting down broken infantry ... nothing could stop out advance. We passed whole batteries of guns, columns of marching troops moving east.' At one point, a bridge over the Dnieper at Terpinye, the appearance of the *Leibstandarte* prompted the Russians to blow the bridge, even though it was crowded with their own men. However, the Waffen-SS soldiers found a ford not far away and managed to get across the river. It seemed nothing could stop the German advance into the Russian heartland.

LEFT: As summer gave way to autumn the rains came. On 17 October 1941 the *Leibstandarte* had taken Tagonrog, followed by Stalino three days later. In this sector of the front it then rained incessantly for several weeks, first slowing and then halting the German advance. Tanks, trucks and artillery pieces sank into the slime, while both men and horses laboured to free the stuck vehicles. Hundreds of horses died from heart strain pulling immobilised hardware.

RIGHT: Russian women feverishly dig anti-tank ditches as the Germans near Moscow. Their efforts were not needed: Despite losing vast amounts of men and equipment, and ceding a massive amount of territory to the Germans, the Red Army was still fighting as the end of 1941 approached. Moreover, the German Army had experienced horrendous losses itself, as had the Waffen-SS. By mid-November, as Army Group Centre struck out for Moscow, Waffen-SS loses amounted to 407 officers and 7930 men killed, 816 officers and 26,299 men wounded, 13 officers and 923 men missing, and four officers and 125 men killed in accidents. The other side of the coin was that during the four months that it had been fighting in Russia, Himmler's legions had earned a military renown they were to retain among both friends and foes for the rest of the war. They had also earned an unenviable reputation for atrocities.

ABOVE: Abandoned German vehicles on the Eastern Front. Hitler's delaying of the attack on Moscow had resulted in spectacular but inconclusive actions in the Baltic states and the Ukraine, but when the orders were given to complete Operation 'Barbarossa' with the capture of Moscow, codenamed 'Typhoon', it was too late in the year. The situation at the front was dire: casualties and sickness were wasting units faster than replacements could reach the frontline, resulting in companies having an average strength of under 50 men, a quarter of their war establishment. In addition, those men still standing had marched nearly 1600km (1000 miles) since 22 June – they had no boots or socks and were physically and mentally exhausted. Horses were dying at a rate of 1000 a day, there were no vehicle spares and the Red Army, which *should* have ceased to exist, was still fighting. The logistical situation for the Waffen-SS was just as dire, but its fighting spirit remained intact. So much so that General Eberhard von Mackensen, commander of III Panzer Corps, wrote an unsolicited letter to Himmler regarding the performance of Hitler's bodyguard. Though it concerns only the *Leibstandarte*, its comments can be equally applied to the other Waffen-SS divisions fighting in Russia at this time. It is worth repeating in full: 'It will perhaps be of some value to you to hear, from the mouth of that commanding general under whom the

Leibstandarte has served during this long and difficult campaign and one who is a member of the army and not the SS, what he and other divisions think about this unit. Herr Reichsführer, I can assure you that the *Leibstandarte* enjoys an outstanding reputation not only with its superiors, but also among its army comrades. Every division wishes it had the *Leibstandarte* as its neighbour, as much during the attack as in defence. Its inner discipline, its cool daredevilry, its cheerful enterprise, its unshakable firmness in a crisis (even when things become difficult or serious), its exemplary toughness, its camaraderie (which deserves special praise) – all these are outstanding and cannot be surpassed. In spite of this, the officer corps maintains a pleasant degree of modesty. A genuine élite formation that I am happy and proud to have under my command and, furthermore, one that I sincerely and hopefully wish to retain! This unrestrained recognition was gained by the *Leibstandarte* entirely on the strength of its own achievements and moreover on the basis of its military ability against an enemy whose courage, toughness, numbers and armaments should not be slighted. The aura which naturally surrounds the Führer's Guard would not have sufficed, here at the front, to allow this recognition to fall into its laps.' Similar praise was forthcoming from other generals, proving that the Waffen-SS had come of age.

CHAPTER NINE

Winter War

The Waffen-SS and the first winter in Russia

The German war machine that had smashed into the Soviet Union in June 1941 was running out of steam as the end of the year rapidly approached.

The Russian summer had consisted of scorching heat, with choking dust and rain turning roads into impassable rivers of mud. But the worst horror was to come: the full fury of the Russian

LEFT: In Russia the Panje horse, a short, stocky beast with great stamina, was used by both sides for transport during the winter months on the Eastern Front.

OPPOSITE: A despatch rider and colleague of the *Wiking* Division try to extract the machine from the mud.

winter. The Germans, dressed in summer uniforms, were caught totally unprepared as temperatures began to plummet. The mechanisms of their guns began to freeze, along with the oil in their engines and sumps. If moisture formed in machine-gun barrels, it turned to ice in the cold and split the barrels when the weapons were fired. Nevertheless, the Germans still hoped to take Moscow before the year ended in one last effort.

OPERATION 'TYPHOON'

Operation 'Typhoon', the codename for the attack on Moscow, began on 4 October, with excellent initial progress. *Das Reich* and the 10th Panzer Division advanced, but then got bogged down with the advent of the autumn rains, only reaching Gzhatsk on 9 October. The *Das Reich* Division was again on the move by mid-October, meeting fierce resistance as it pushed towards Moscow. After crossing the River Moskv, the division took Mozhaisk on 18 October, but the weather had worsened and supplies of ammunition were running low. The first of countless cases of frostbite were encountered as the temperature plummeted dramatically. XLVI Panzer Corps' advance continued with a thrust towards Istra on 18 November. After fierce fighting, the remaining tanks of the 10th Panzer and *Das Reich* Divisions penetrated the town on 26 November.

The German High Command still hoped to take Moscow, but with every day that passed the weather became more severe: daytime temperatures hovered around minus 34 degrees Celsius (minus 30 degrees Fahrenheit), while those at night could fall as low as minus 44 degrees Celsius (minus 47 degrees Fahrenheit). Both the *Deutschland* and *Der Führer* Regiments had to be regrouped due to manpower losses. The freezing temperatures were also taking a toll on vehicles: all but seven of the tanks of the 10th Panzer Division had been rendered inoperable.

THE GERMAN ADVANCE STOPS DEAD IN THE SNOW

The great German assault against Moscow was grinding slowly to a halt. After six months of continuous fighting, mounting casualties, horrendous weather and supply lines that were over stretched, German forces were close to the brink of collapse. Although the very gates of Moscow had been rattled by the Germans, the Red Army, albeit having been forced back, was able to establish a reserve to the east of the Soviet capital. The Moscow city tramcar system terminus was reached on 4 December 1941 by the *Das Reich*'s reconnaissance battalion, before the weather forced a pause in the attack. This was to be the farthest point reached in the assault on Moscow, for on 6 December 1941 around one and a half million Soviet troops – 17 armies – hurled themselves against the exhausted Germans.

LEFT: Waffen-SS soldiers in Russia, December 1941. The first winter in Russia came as a shock to the Germans. A member of the *Leibstandarte* wrote: 'We have to strip the fallen, theirs and ours, for warm clothing. I don't think I will ever be warm again, and our tame Ivans say that this is a mild winter.'

The first major Soviet counteroffensive on the Eastern Front tore huge gaps in the German line. On 9 December, the order to retreat was given, and *Das Reich* began to retire. Farther north, in what was to be called the Demyansk Pocket, the *Totenkopf* Division, plus five other German divisions, were destined to find themselves imprisoned.

ZHUKOV'S COUNTEROFFENSIVE

On 5 December 1941, the Red Army's fresh, well-equipped divisions were unleashed against Army Group Centre. The Germans lines buckled, and the generals wanted to withdraw to Smolensk. However, Hitler ordered every German soldier to stand firm: any form of withdrawal was out of the question. On this occasion Hitler's inflexibility helped to avert a total rout of the German armies before Moscow, gradually the German defences firmed up, and the front had stabilised in the central sector by the end of January.

In the north the Soviet objective was to encircle and annihilate the German 16th Army. Army Group North and Army Group Centre would then have a vast space between them, which would permit the Red Army to flow through. The southern shore of Lake Ilmen was the intended route for the Soviet 11th and 34th Armies and the 1st Shock Army. Aiming to sweep around the lower edge of Lake Seliger, the 16th Shock Army would also join the attack.

German forces in the north had the advantage of knowing when arranging their defence strategies that they were to experience heavy pressure. During December they therefore concentrated on strengthening their defence lines. Two German corps – II Corps and X Corps – were positioned between Lake Ilmen and Lake Seliger, and to the west along the River Lovat. The *Totenkopf* Division was part of this force, and dug itself into the Valdai Hills.

Under cover of a fierce blizzard, the second phase of the Russian winter counter-offensive was launched during the night of 7-8 January 1942. The Red Army attacked along the whole of Army Group North's southern flank. The *Totenkopf*

Division's neighbours, the 30th and 290th Infantry Divisions, received the full brunt of the Soviet 11th, 34th and 1st Shock Armies' attacks, and were all but annihilated.

Then the Red Army implemented a plan that, if it succeeded, would trap the German 16th Army. The 11th Army wheeled south at Staraya Russa into the rear of II corps. From the shores of Lake Seliger, driving west with the intention of linking up with the 11th and 1st Shock Armies, the 16th Shock Army turned north along the line of the River Lovat.

The *Totenkopf* Division was divided and deployed to various crisis points. To strengthen the 16th Army's flanks, two of its infantry battalions were sent to Demyansk, while its reconnaissance battalions were deployed at Staraya Russa, which they were ordered to hold at all costs.

HITLER'S ORDER – NO RETREAT!

The situation had become critical by 12 January 1942. Field Marshal Leeb believed the best course of action was to withdraw both his corps over the River Lovat and form a new defensive line. The worried field marshal was certain it would be akin to a death sentence if the 16th Army was to stand firm. Leeb asked permission to withdraw, Hitler refused, ordering his troops to hold fast. An outraged Leeb asked to be relieved of his command, Hitler agreed. In his place he appointed Colonel-General Küchler on 17 January.

Meanwhile, the two German corps were being squeezed into a pocket at Demyansk On 20 January the Russians broke through along the River Lovat. German units were now isolated on the west and east banks of the river – it was only a matter of time before the encirclement of the 16th Army became inevitable. Heavy fighting continued for three weeks as the Soviets gradually closed the ring. On 8 February, 40km (25 miles) west of Demyansk, units of the Soviet 11th and 1st Shock Armies linked up on the River Lovat; the Soviet ring had closed firmly around II and X Corps, trapping the 12th, 30th, 32nd, 123rd and 290th Infantry Divisions, plus the remainder of the *Totenkopf*. The equivalent of 15 Russian infantry divisions, supported by armoured units, surrounded

95,000 men and 20,000 horses in the pocket. With the assurance of Göring that the pocket could be supplied by air, Hitler reiterated his order of no withdrawal. The trapped German divisions were instructed to hold their positions until a new front west of the River Lovat was established, from where a relief attack could be launched.

TOTENKOPF POSITIONS INSIDE THE DEMYANSK POCKET

As the Soviet ring finally closed, General Brockdorff-Ahlefeldt took command of the troops within the pocket. The remaining *Totenkopf* Division units were split into two battle groups, which included army personnel. Eicke was ordered to defend the southwest sector of the pocket, which involved the protection of a large network of villages and their interlinking roads. The German units on the eastern and western banks of the River Lovat had had a corridor driven between them; this had to be stopped from being widened at all costs. SS-Oberführer Max Simon commanded the second battle group that faced the Soviet 34th Army in the northeastern edge of the pocket.

The Russians dropped incendiary bombs on buildings to deny any form of shelter to the *Totenkopf*'s troops, who were fighting in waist-high snow and sub-zero temperatures. In a number of places Soviet forces had penetrated the German lines by late February. These had produced their own little pockets as individual villages were cut off and surrounded.

Red Army artillery incessantly pounded Eicke's men, resulting in steadily mounting losses among the Waffen-SS grenadiers. The situation on the ground became so confused that *Totenkopf* troops were strafed by their own side, and Luftwaffe aircraft dropped supplies behind Soviet lines.

Eicke appealed directly to Himmler for replacements, now fearing for the very survival of his mauled division. When Himmler was eventually able to muster several hundred replacements that could be flown into the pocket, the Luftwaffe insisted that its supply flights did not have the capacity to carry them.

Eicke's men held on desperately until the spring thaws came in mid-March, when the Soviet attacks began to tail off. Lieutenant-General Walter von Seydlitz-Kurzbach assembled a relief force on the west bank of the River Lovat. The Demyansk Pocket was relieved on 20 April. However, the *Totenkopf* Division's ordeal was far from being over. The remnants of Eicke's once mighty division was kept in the line to ensure that the German corridor was held open. Leave and refitting would have to wait.

BELOW: The lucky ones: Luftwaffe personnel in special warm winter clothing in Russia. On the left is Oberstleutnant Othmar Wolfan, who is on an inspection tour of installations on the Eastern Front. The Waffen-SS was able to organise winter clothing for its men much quicker than did the army.

LEFT: Huddled together in an effort to prevent heat loss, a Waffen-SS motorcycle team take a break. Their machine is fitted with snow chains to provide extra grip and they are wrapped in winter clothing, but the cold is still numbing. One SS lieutenant-colonel, reflecting on the first winter in Russia stated: 'How did we cope with the abnormal climatic conditions experienced during the winter of 1941-42? Quite simply, we acclimatised quickly. Those who did not, died.' Tens of thousands did not acclimatise.

BELOW: As well as its freezing winter, the Soviet Union was littered with marshlands. This posed a two-fold problem for the Germans. First, mobility was greatly reduced. Large swamp holes could completely swallow a man or vehicle. Second, the residents of the marshes were able to guide Russian units cut off by the German advance to safe refuges, from where they could launch attacks against the vulnerable German rear areas and communications. Operating in swamps was a nightmare for German troops, not least because of the mosquitoes that made life a misery. Note the plank walkway to cross the marsh.

LEFT: Mud – the bane of the soldier on the Eastern Front. It is often said that in the East the cold killed quickly but mud broke men spiritually and mentally. Whole armies ground to a standstill. In October 1941, for example, the *Wiking* Division, trying to overtake enemy units near Wolnowacha, was slowed to a snail's pace by 14 days of rain, which turned the area into a sea of mud, allowing the Russians to regroup.

BELOW: A German half-track extracts a lorry from the mud. The Germans soon discovered that tracked and semi-tracked vehicles were invaluable in Russia. When the rains came wheeled transport was either pushed off the roads or towed through the worst stretches by tracked vehicles. Main roads were restricted to give priority to vehicles carrying ammunition and fuel, and in extremely muddy conditions all wheeled vehicles were removed from the road, leaving the way clear for tracked and half-tracked transport. But even the tracked vehicles often got stuck, or simply broke down. The effect on the troops was debilitating. The *Das Reich* Division was a case in point. By the end of October 1941, after fighting on poor terrain, without hot meals and in terrible weather, the division's soldiers were exhausted. They were suffering from frostbite and stomach illnesses, and a divisional report to Berlin recommended: 'a rest of several days where possible in warm and heated billets is essential for the success of any new attack.' The report was ignored.

DEMYANSK

The tenacity of the *Totenkopf* Division in the Demyansk Pocket in 1942 prevented a total German rout in northern Russia, but success was bought at a terrible price.

RIGHT: On the lookout for the next Russian attack on the edge of the Demyansk Pocket. By the beginning of February 1942, the *Totenkopf* Division had ben split into two battle groups, which were deployed in the two most hard-pressed areas inside the pocket. With 15 Red Army divisions surrounding the 95,000 German troops inside the pocket it seemed inevitable that it would be eradicated. However, Hitler named the pocket 'Fortress Demyansk' and forbade any breakout attempt. This suited the men of the *Totenkopf*, whose fighting spirit during this time was summarised by the historian Charles Sydnor: 'For Eicke and his SS men, there was no questioning Hitler's order to stand and fight to the last man. This was the kind of order the hard-bitten *Totenkopf* soldiers understood best, and the type of assignment for which they had few peers on the Eastern Front.' One thing in the *Totenkopf*'s favour was that Eicke's men were able to fight more effectively than their army counterparts in the severe weather due to them having ample winter clothing. This was from the massive warehouse of confiscated goods in Riga, which was controlled by the SS for use in northern Russia. Indeed, Eicke's men were soon complaining that the winter clothing was too bulky, which reduced the mobility of the wearer, and restricted visibility.

LEFT: A pause between Russian attacks. The Red Army's efforts to annihilate the pocket occurred during the last week of February 1942. By this time the *Totenkopf* Division had been divided into two battle groups, and Eicke's battle group, deployed along the western edge of the pocket, was pounded mercilessly with heavy artillery fire. At the same time, the Russians increased the scale and intensity of their infantry and armoured attacks. But, against all the odds, the Waffen-SS soldiers held.

ABOVE: To deny any sort of shelter to the *Totenkopf* soldiers, the Red Army Air Force dropped incendiary bombs on any buildings inside the pocket. The fighting became so fierce that Russian attacks were stopped only when the SS grenadiers had wiped out all the attackers. Such combat resulted in a high attrition rate for the Waffen-SS. By the third week of February, Eicke's battle group, which was defending a 12.8km (eight-mile) front, consisted of 36 officers, 191 NCOs and 1233 other ranks. The only order Eicke gave was to stand firm, believing that superior will and fanatical resistance would eventually destroy the Russian offensives. In this way he drove his men to the limit of their endurance.

BELOW: At the end of February 1942, the German lines in the pocket had been penetrated in a number of places by Russian forces. The few German tanks that remained in use went to reinforce those units which were being pressed the most. Eicke's men had been forced into a number of isolated pockets as individual villages were cut off and surrounded. Losses mounted dramatically. The wounded could no longer be evacuated to the hospital at Demyansk, but still the *Totenkopf* Division fought on. By mid-March Eicke's men had suffered losses of 7000 men, and when it was finally taken out of the line in October 1942, it had only 6400 soldiers left alive. At the beginning of 'Barbarossa' the *Totenkopf* had over 18,000 men.

ABOVE: Soldiers of the *Totenkopf* Division haul supplies through the snow using mules. Following the easing of Russian attacks against the Demyansk Pocket on 20 March, Eicke issued estimates that claimed his division had inflicted 22,279 casualties on Red Army units. As for the condition of his own troops, in April an SS doctor submitted a report to Max Simon, the division's second-in-command, that some of the *Totenkopf*'s soldiers were in such poor physical shape that they resembled concentration camp inmates (with hindsight, a most revealing comment in more ways than one), the result of insufficient food, the intense cold and inadequate shelter. Medically most of them were not capable of further combat.

BELOW: Skis were an effective method of cross-country movement across the frozen terrain. The experience of battle for individual Waffen-SS soldiers in the Russian winter left a deep impression. One *Leibstandarte* grenadier wrote of a Russian attack near the Don in November 1941: 'They came in in masses so great as to numb the sense. We drove them off, and when they had gone back across the ice the whole area to both flanks and in front of our positions was carpeted with dead. They were dead all right ... the wounded die quickly; the blood freezes as it leaves the body and a sort of shock sets in which kills. Light wounds that heal in three days in summer kill you in winter.'

LEFT AND BELOW: The Medal for the Winter Campaign in Russia, 1941-42. The sarcastic nickname given to this award by the troops at the front was the 'Frozen Meat Medal' (their gallows humour was prompted by scenes such as below left, where Waffen-SS soldiers are pulling the frozen corpse of one of their comrades so he can receive a proper burial). The medal was introduced by Hitler on 26 May 1942 for the campaign in Russia. The period of qualification for the award was from 15 November 1941 to 15 April 1942, and by the order of the Armed Forces High Command (OKW) consideration for rendering the award ceased on 4 September 1944. It was to be worn on the medal bar, and even though it was a campaign medal it took precedence over the War Merit Medal. The criteria for the award were as follows: to have been engaged in combat in the theatre of operations for two weeks; to have spent 60 days continuously in the combat theatre; to have been wounded in the combat zone; or to have suffered frost-bite (frost-bite in Russia could be severe, and thus explains why a wound badge or medal could be awarded for a non-military wound). Luftwaffe personnel also qualified for this award if they had spent 30 days over enemy territory. It was designed by SS-Unterscharführer Ernst Kraus.

ABOVE: A German horse-drawn supply column makes it way to the front. The Russian counteroffensive that began in December 1941 had precipitated a crisis for the German Army in the East. Attacking across 1600km (1000 miles) of front, the Red Army had cleared the Moscow and Tula regions, parts of the Kalinin, Smolensk, Orel and Kursk regions had been partially cleared, and some 60 towns had been liberated. In some places the German Army had been pushed back 320km (200 miles). The Germans had lost a colossal amount of men and war material: 500,000 men, 1300 tanks, 2500 guns and over 1500 vehicles. The Waffen-SS had itself had suffered horrendous casualties, losing over 8000 dead and 28,000 wounded even before the Russian offensive, and the *Das Reich* Division had lost 60 per cent of its fighting strength. Granted Himmler's legions had performed admirably, and had obeyed Hitler's order to stand firm to the letter (which was to have unfortunate results in the long term, in that the Führer believed the German Army's survival in Russia in the first winter had been down to his judgement; in future years his 'no retreat' fixation was to have disastrous results on the Eastern front as he stubbornly clung on to every metre of ground while the Red Army swept past his units), but the losses in men, particularly officers, had been appalling. On the other hand, the Waffen-SS's performance had not gone unnoticed by Hitler, and as a result its military credibility had improved enormously.

ABOVE: Grenadiers of the *Totenkopf* Division during the early phase of the fighting in the Demyansk Pocket. Note the buildings are still standing, a situation that was to change when Red Army artillery reduced any structures in the pocket to rubble in an effort to deny the Germans shelter.

ABOVE: A Panzer II on the Eastern Front, January 1942. By February the Russian counteroffensive had slackened, and by March the Germans had stablised the front. Their losses since the start of 'Barbarossa' amounted to over three million casualties, some 35 per cent of the force committed. Around 200,000 men were dead, while the Waffen-SS had suffered losses of 43,000. It was obvious that the quota of native German recruits for the Waffen-SS as allotted by OKW would be inadequate to replace these losses. Foreigners would therefore have to be found to fill the gaps.

RIGHT: A German squad in Russia, February 1942. One SS-Hauptsturmführer wrote of this period: 'It was those defensive battles of the winter of 1941-42 which I shall always remember for the sheer beauty of the fighting. Many of us died horribly, some even as cowards, but for those who lived even for a short period out there, it was well worth the dreadful suffering and danger ... we were not concerned for ourselves or even for Germany, but lived entirely for the next clash, the next engagement with the enemy.'

CHAPTER TEN

Metamorphosis

Reorganisation and expansion of the Waffen-SS

The second year of the war in Russia, 1942, witnessed the growth and reorganisation of the Waffen-SS, seeing the birth of the mighty SS panzer and panzergrenadier divisions. The Waffen-SS cadre divisions had become fully motorised by 1942, but as each had a panzer regiment they were in fact panzer divisions in all but name.

Before the end of 1942, however, they were officially redesignated as SS-Panzer-Grenadier-Divisionen (armoured infantry divisions), and soon after their infantry regiments were designated SS-Panzer-Grenadier-Regimenter. The general background to the origins of the first divisions of the Waffen-SS, and how they were created early in World War II from the full-time paramilitary formations of the SS already in existence, gives an insight into the development and expansion that now occurred.

THE WAFFEN-SS CASTS ITS RECRUITMENT NET WIDE

The nucleus of the first of these divisions was the *Leibstandarte SS Adolf Hitler*, the Führer's personal bodyguard. The 2nd SS Division was formed from the SS-Verfügungstruppe (SS Special Purpose Troops), becoming the *Das Reich* Division. The 3rd SS Division was provided by elements of the SS-Totenkopfverbände (SS Death's Head Regiments), with the German police forming the fourth of Himmler's divisions. The Death's Head Regiments that had not been used for the creation of what was to become the *Totenkopf* became the cadre for others, such as the 6th SS Gebirgs Division *Nord*, 8th SS Kavallerie Division *Florian Geyer* and 18th SS Freiwilligen-Panzergrenadier-Division *Horst Wessel*. Those of German blood who lived outside the Third Reich were known as Volksdeutsche, and so many volunteered for service in the Waffen-SS that whole divisions were constructed around them, the best known being the 7th SS-Freiwilligen-Gebirgs Division *Prinz Eugen*.

Following German conquests in western and northern Europe, volunteers from the so-called 'Nordic' countries signed up for service, being grouped into Germanic Waffen-SS divisions. Eventually, non-Germanic western Europeans were also grouped into divisions, eroding the grandiose racial requirements for SS membership set down by Himmler. The final irony was the creation of whole SS divisions from what were formally believed by the Nazi theorists to be 'inferior races'.

THE WAFFEN-SS'S CHANGING ORDER OF BATTLE

The fortunes of war produced structural changes within the divisions of the Waffen-SS: there was a continual change in the divisional orders of battle, and units were redesignated during their comparatively short lives, especially when their parent divisions were partially or fully motorised. For example, a regiment could find itself at first designated a schützen-regiment (rifle regiment), then an infanterie-regiment (infantry regiment), next a grenadier-regiment (grenadier regiment) and finally a panzergrenadier-regiment (armoured infantry regiment). Units were transferred from one division to another and redesignated, whereas others were reclassified *en masse* in the Waffen-SS and Wehrmacht.

Waffen-SS divisions could be grouped into corps, as in the army, which if necessary could then be formed into an army.

LEFT: Flemish SS volunteers being addressed on Hitler's self-styled 'crusade against Bolshevism'. Reichsführer-SS Himmler was very keen to attract suitably Germanic volunteers for the Waffen-SS, stating: 'We must attract all the Nordic blood in the world to us, and so deprive our enemies of it.'

As with most large military organisations, the Waffen-SS established a number of corps headquarters during the war. These had their respective corps troops to provide their field divisions with tactical leadership. At first two divisions formed a corps, but after a while they were made up of whatever was available. With the constant movement of mobile divisions and the demands of war, SS corps could comprise troops who were purely SS, a combination of SS and army, or even just army elements. The number of corps troops varied from corps to corps, and generally those corps which were formed first were more powerful. And sometimes the designation of corps was a mockery.

EICKE'S GHOST CORPS

In northern Russian in early 1942, the remnants of Eicke's once mighty *Totenkopf* Division should have been withdrawn from the front. However, the military situation meant the *Totenkopf* Division's ordeal was far from over. Now in a dreadful physical state and in desperate need of a refit, Hitler ordered that it remain in the Demyansk salient, its objective being to hold open the corridor at all costs. The army and SS troops within the western part of the salient were combined into a new corps under the command of Theodor Eicke. In reality the strength of this formation was only half that of a single division. Eicke's pessimism concerning the *Totenkopf* Division's plight was communicated to Colonel-General Busch, who was very sympathetic, urging an immediate intake of at least 5000 fresh troops if it was to continue its tasks. However, it received only 3000 replacements from Reichsführer-SS Himmler.

The Red Army went onto the offensive in May 1942, and the corridor was held open with great difficulty. Russian attacks intensified as spring gave way to summer, which greatly weakened Eicke's corps. In mid-June when Eicke, physically exhausted, was ordered to take a period of rest, SS-Oberführer Max Simon assumed temporary command. At the end of his spell of leave Eicke was ordered to report to Führer Headquarters at Rastenburg, where he was decorated by Hitler personally with the Oakleaves to his Knight's Cross, becoming the 88th recipient. Eicke took the opportunity to tell Hitler of the appalling state of his remaining troops. The Führer refused to allow the *Totenkopf* Division to be withdrawn from the Demyansk salient, but he did promise Eicke to make it a fully rebuilt panzergrenadier division, complete with its own tank battalion, when it was withdrawn. Until such time Eicke was to remain on leave.

A NEW DIVISION FORGED IN THE CAULDRON OF BATTLE

By early July 1942, severe Soviet pressure was being exerted on the *Totenkopf*, and SS-Oberführer Simon desperately pleaded for the withdrawal of the division before it was destroyed, which he believed was now only a matter of time. Eicke, reviewing Simon's reports, pleaded again for the division's withdrawal. But Hitler insisted that it must stand firm until the salient had been sufficiently strengthened to withstand future enemy attacks (it was estimated that X Corps would need a further 6-8 weeks before it could be put into the line). On 17 July, massive Soviet assaults were unleashed upon the exhausted *Totenkopf* troops. The defenders of Vasilyevschina were wiped out to a man when it was captured on 18 July. Against this red torrent, and in contradiction to direct orders from his army superiors, SS-Oberführer Simon refused to launch an immediate counterattack. If the army required the task to be done, he suggested, then they should do it themselves. So the 8th Light Division attacked instead of the *Totenkopf*. It failed to oust the Russians from their positions, and in the process suffered heavy losses.

Soviet attempts to crush the salient continued, though the weather had deteriorated. In thigh-deep glutinous mud, both sides fought for several days until 30 July, when the Soviet attacks withered. Just as well, for the SS troops were on their last legs. The results of long periods of fighting in what can only be described as swamp conditions were becoming apparent: diseases spread like wildfire, the soldiers succumbing easily to dysentery, pneumonia and many other racking complaints. Registering his anger, Eicke once again demanded of Hitler that his division be withdrawn at once to rest and undergo a complete refit. If the Führer thought otherwise, then he should allow Eicke to return to die with his men at the front. Hitler, unsurprisingly, refused.

RELIEF AT LAST FOR THE *TOTENKOPF*

On 6 August, the northern and southern edges of the corridor came under heavy attacks from the Soviet 11th Army and I Guards Corps. The *Totenkopf* Division once again suffered debilitating casualties, and in a final effort its non-combatant personnel – clerks, medics, military police and even the cooks – joined their comrades and filled the trenches. They stood awaiting what they knew would be certain death.

But the *Totenkopf* Division was saved from being overrun when the heavens opened and torrential rain fell. For two days all military operations ceased, and over the next week or so the *Totenkopf* soldiers were able to summon up enough strength to keep the enemy at bay. But now a mere 7000 men, most of them non-combatant troops, made up the so-called corps.

On 25 August more Russian attacks occurred. The *Totenkopf* Division was separated into numerous isolated pockets, but all the assaults were fought off successfully. Simon's command determinedly held its positions, but in just a few hours over 1000 men were lost. The battered *Totenkopf*

RIGHT: The so-called Reichszeugmeisterei (RZM) code controlled the manufacture of all Nazi Party items. The organisation itself was based at the Brown House in Munich and party headquarters in Berlin. As can be seen here, all RZM items carried a logo and serial number.

Division now had Eicke back, but each week he had to return to Germany to oversee preparations for its rebuilding.

The *Totenkopf* was finally withdrawn in October 1942, where it was integrated into a new, powerful corps. The headquarters for this Corps SS-Generalkommando (mot) was ordered by Hitler on 13 May 1942 and authorised on 28 May. The formation of the corps was ordered on 9 July 1942 to take place in Germany. It was then transferred to northern France later that month to integrate with the SS infantry divisions reforming as armoured divisions after having been on the Eastern Front. Its headquarters was redesignated as SS-General-Kommando (Panzer) on 1 June 1942. The corps was formed from the *Leibstandarte*, *Das Reich* and *Totenkopf* Divisions. They were all immensely powerful, being reconstructed and reformed as panzergrenadier divisions, though in reality they were panzer divisions and should be designated so. Tempered in the white-heat of combat in Russia, composed of battle-hardened veterans imbued with the fighting spirit of the Waffen-SS and lavishly equipped with the latest heavy weapons, this new corps – I SS Panzer Corps – gave Hitler hope that he could smash the Red Army in 1943.

During the second week in January 1943 therefore, at the Führer's express order, this new corps was transported to the Eastern Front, employing all the speed it could muster, and with top priority being given to its divisions regarding rail and road transport to the front. The *Der Führer* Regiment, *Das Reich* Division, was the first unit of the corps to reach the front. A new chapter in the history of the Waffen-SS was about to begin.

THE PRAETORIANS REBORN

The fighting spirit displayed by the premier divisions of the Waffen-SS in Russia in 1941-42 led to their reorganisation as panzer divisions, among the strongest the Wehrmacht had.

LEFT: The sleeve band of the 1st SS Panzer Division *Leibstandarte*, with aluminium thread edges and light brown, machine-embroidered Sütterlin script, which was introduced in early 1940. The German Army had used cuff bands and titles for some time, a practice that was continued by the Nazis. Their first major one was the 'Stosstrupp Adolf Hitler 1923' to commemorate the former Stosstrupp men.

BELOW: As early as January 1942 Hitler had decreed that the *Leibstandarte* and *Das Reich* Divisions should each have a tank battalion, and by the end of May the *Totenkopf* and *Wiking* Divisions were also allocated tank battalions. By the end of 1942 the *Leibstandarte*, *Das Reich* and *Totenkopf* Divisions had been fully equipped as panzergrenadier divisions (though by the time they reached the front in early 1943 they were in reality panzer divisions). Hitler ordered the creation of two new armoured SS divisions in December 1943 – *Frundsberg* and *Hohenstaufen* – and authorised one raised from Hitler Youth in early 1943. These units were allocated the best military equipment available, such as this Tiger tank.

LEFT: BeVo-pattern cuff bands for the *Das Reich*, *Hohenstaufen* and *Totenkopf* Divisions, introduced in 1943. 'BeVo' is the name given to the process of weaving insignia by the so-called Jacquard method. The term 'BeVo' comes from the trade name found on much of the woven insignia of many Third Reich military and political organisations. 'Be' stands for Beteiligung, meaning 'partnership', while the 'Vo' stands for Vorsteher. The amalgamation of the firms of Lucas Vorsteher of Lenneper Strasse 50 and Ewelda Vorsteher of Krenz Strasse 72, both from Wuppertal, created a new logo: BeVo-Wuppertal.

RIGHT: Machine-woven cuff band for the 10th SS Panzer Division *Frundsberg*, BeVo pattern, introduced in 1943. On 1 June 1943, the division was named 10th SS Panzergrenadier Division *Karl der Grosse*, but no cuff band was ever awarded bearing this title. The division was renamed *Frundsberg* on 3 October 1943, and a cuff band authorised bearing this title. The machine-woven cuff band for the 12th SS Panzer Division *Hitlerjugend* is also of BeVo pattern, and was authorised for wear on 24 June 1943, but the machine-embroidered cuff band for the 5th SS Panzer Division *Wiking*, with silver-grey thread letter and aluminium thread edges, is in the RZM style.

LEFT: Waffen-Brigadeführer Bronislav Vladislavovich Kaminski, a Russian who was the son of a Polish father and German mother. Born in St Petersburg, he was a chemical engineer by profession. Imprisoned by the Soviets for five years for the crimes of being a 'foreigner', bourgeois intellectual and potential dissident, he was released only months before the German invasion of June 1941. Having no love for the government in Moscow, he was one of thousands who offered their services to the German invaders. Kaminski, who spoke German fluently, threw himself wholeheartedly behind the Nazi cause. A brilliant, though autocratic, organiser, his only failure was an attempt to form a Russian Nazi Party. In January 1942, the town of Lokot fell under the jurisdiction of the 2nd Panzer Army. It stood on the edge of the Bryansk Forest, about halfway between Orec and Kursk, central Russia. Under Kaminski's rule it became a model of self-sufficiency, having its own newspapers, hospitals, banks and tax system. The food supplies never failed to be delivered to the Wehrmacht on time, and the Germans found they only needed a small liaison staff in Lokot. Kaminski's empire soon expanded: the original self-defence force of 500 men had grown into a brigade of 10,000 by September 1943, organised into five infantry regiments, an artillery detachment of 36 field guns, an armoured unit made up of 24 captured Russian T-34 tanks, plus various support units. This force was titled 'The Russian Liberation People's Army' (RONA). However, by this time the Germans were in retreat in the East, and so RONA was removed to Ratibor on the Polish-Czech border. Now comprising 15,000 men, it was accompanied by 10,500 civilians and 1500 cows.

RIGHT: A RONA arm shield. This comprised a black cross on a white background, outlined in red. Above this, in off-white, are the letters RONA (though being in Cyrillic this becomes POHA), the whole design having a field-grey background. The official version of this shield is the Cross of St George, a Czarist military decoration, in black on a white background; above this, in yellow on a black frame, are the letters RONA. In March 1944 RONA was renamed a Volksheer Brigade (People's Brigade), and in July it was accepted into the Waffen-SS as SS Assault Brigade RONA. Kaminski was granted a commission as a Waffen-Brigadeführer, though his men were not regarded as being fit for frontline duty and were sent to Hungary for further training (it is interesting that the urgencies of war had resulted in these Russians no longer being termed 'sub-human'). When, in August 1944, the Polish Home Army began its abortive rising in Warsaw, one regiment of 1700 men under Lieutenant-Colonel Vrolov was detached from the brigade to assist in the suppression of the revolt. It arrived on 5 August, but was withdrawn three weeks later on the orders of Erich von dem Bach-Zelewski due to its atrocious conduct and general lack of discipline. Kaminski himself was arrested by the SS and charged with looting, found guilty and shot by firing squad.

BELOW: The Russian defector Andrei Vlassov (second from left), who formed a Russian Liberation Army (ROA) from Russian prisoners. When Vlassov met Himmler he found the Reichsführer-SS remarkably affable and accommodating. Himmler proposed the immediate formation of a Committee for the Liberation of the Peoples of Russia, which would be granted the status of a provisional government once the Germans were again in control of a large area of Soviet territory (this was in late 1944). The committee would then be allowed to raise an army of five divisions, two of which were to be activated immediately. It never happened. but does illustrate how the realities of war had totally eroded Himmler's racial policies.

RIGHT: Three young Romanian SS Volksdeutche (ethnic Germans living outside Germany's borders) volunteers in the mountains of Yugoslavia. They are receiving hot rations from the mobile cook house. Many Volksdeutsche were farmers and artisans, and often father and son belonged to same unit. As early as 1940 Romanian Volksdeutsche were being trained for service with the Waffen-SS. In May of that year, for example, 1000 had been recruited and by July were beginning to arrive at the SS training centre in Prague. At first most Volksdeutsche recruits were sent to existing Waffen-SS units as replacements. Many of them spoke a corrupted form of German, which caused problems of command.

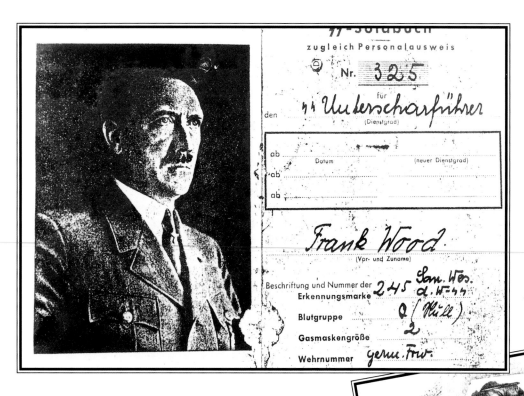

LEFT: An SS-Soldbuch (pay-book). Carrying a picture of Adolf Hitler, it is made out to SS-Unterscharführer Frank Wood, alias Francis MacLardy, a pharmacist who was called up for British service in July 1939. In May 1940 he was in France as part of the Royal Medical Army Corps, and on the 31st was captured at Wormhoudt, the scene of an SS atrocity. He later joined the British Free Corps, a small SS unit.

LEFT: A young volunteer in the 14th Waffen-Grenadier Division der SS *Galicia*, recruited from the western Ukraine. The photo is dated 3 April 1944 and is accredited as his first day. An appeal for volunteers was issued on 28 April 1943, some 70,000 men coming forward. This was more than the 14,000 required to form a division, and so the surplus was absorbed into the German police to form five new police divisions.

ABOVE: Frank Wood, who was the author of several British Free Corps recruiting pamphlets. These reiterated the international aspect of the fight against Bolshevism: 'We are fighting with the best of Europe's youth to preserve our European civilisation and our common cultural heritage from the menace of Jewish Communism. MAKE NO MISTAKE ABOUT IT! Europe includes England.' The appeal fell on deaf ears, the unit numbering under 100.

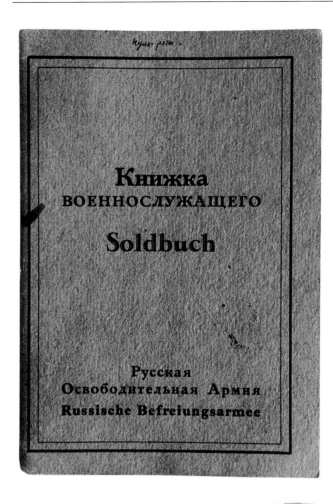

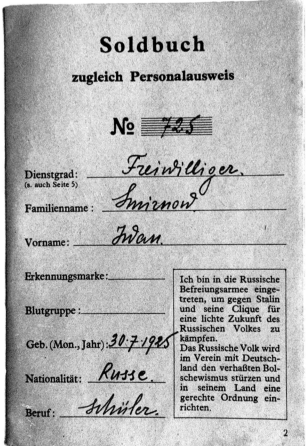

LEFT: The front cover of a Russische Befreiungsarmee Soldbuch (Russian Liberation Army pay-book). It is green with the title in both German and Cyrillic letters. Vlassov had been a Soviet general who had surrendered following an abortive attempt to relieve Leningrad. Bitter at Stalin's desertion of him and his troops, he was a willing puppet of the Germans. He headed the Russian National Committee, which called on Russians to join the movement for a 'new Europe'. At the beginning of 1943 Vlassov's formation assumed the title Russian Liberation Army, or ROA – *Russkaia Osvobodit Armiia*. Despite the grand title, his 'army' was never to number more than two divisions, and by the end of the war in Europe his formation totalled only 18,000 men.

LEFT: The inside of a Russische Befreiungsarmee Soldbuch. It lists the owner as Volunteer Ivan Sminov, with his date of birth being 30 June 1925. By mid-1944 Himmler was making distinctions between 'sub-human' Slavs in Russia and the 'superior elements in the Russian nation'. Satisfied that his racial guidelines were intact, he could thus explain the thousands of Russian recruits who were wearing SS insignia.

ABOVE: A page taken from a pay-book of Russian in German service. Hitler categorically forbade the use of Russians by the Wehrmacht, but the dire military situation in the East after Kursk meant they were recruited on a vast scale. Thousands were enlisted in the Waffen-SS, for anti-partisan operations at first, but then for frontline duties as the German war machine desperately tried to halt the Red Army in 1943-45.

ABOVE: Himmler with SS-Gruppenführer Dr Otto Wächter (right), who was Governor of Galicia (the German name for the western Ukraine) from 1941 until 1944. He wished to raise a Ukrainian SS division, a proposal accepted by Himmler in March 1943, though only for the raising of a police regiment.

However, German reverses in the East meant the regiment was soon expanded into a military division. On the left is SS-Brigadeführer Fritz Freitag, who commanded the Galician division until 27 April 1945. His arrogant attitude towards his men did much to undo Wächter's work.

RIGHT: Himmler awards the first Germanische Leisttungsrune (German Proficiency Runes Badge) to 95 Dutch and German winners at the training school of the Dutch SS at Avegoor near Arnhem. At the end of the ceremony he praised the achievements of the Dutch SS, and the *Westland* Regiment in particular. He then ceremonially raised the Dutch Volunteer Legion to a grenadier brigade, SS-Grenadierbrigade *Nederland*. The Dutch were among the best foreign recruits serving in the Waffen-SS.

LEFT: A foreign Knight's Cross winner: SS-Unterscharführer Remy Schrynen, a Flemish volunteer, with his anti-tank gun on the Eastern Front. A member of the *Langemarck* Brigade, in March 1944 his unit was fighting off a Soviet tank attack in northern Russia. Soon Schrynen was alone, but he stayed at his post, loading and firing his gun. In a dramatic firefight he destroyed three Josef Stalin and four T-34 tanks, though his gun was then blown up by another tank. Schrynen, wounded, was later rescued during a counterattack.

BELOW: SS-Unterscharführer der Reserve Remy Schrynen, a Flemish member of the Waffen-SS, some of whose exploits are listed above. Soldiers like Schrynen were a godsend to Himmler, who paraded their achievements as evidence of a united 'Germanic' Europe fighting Bolshevism on the Eastern Front.

Men like Schrynen fought gallantly in Himmler's service. His awards are impressive: 1939 Iron Cross Second Class, 1939 Iron Cross First Class, Knight's Cross, Infantry Assault Badge Silver Class, Wound Badge 1939 Gold Class, Tollenaere Commemorative Badge, and VNV Golden Party Badge.

LEFT: Mass rally of the *Dietsche Militie* (DM), the 'Black Brigade', held in Brussels. This was the voluntary 'Storm Troop' of the *Vlaamsch Nationaal Verbond* (VNV) of Flanders. The banner in the middle carries the Commemorative Badges of Jois van Severen and the 'Black Brigade' commander, Reimond Tollenaere. The DM was to become a recruiting ground for the Waffen-SS, especially when the invasion of Russia took place. Shortly afterwards, the formation of a Flemish legion was announced, and on 6 August 1941 a draft of 405 young Flemings, mostly ex-Black Brigade, joined up, including Tollenaere. The Flemish recruits found discipline in the German-controlled legion harsher than expected. This prompted many complaints to VNV Headquarters, which were forwarded to Himmler (who eventually was to issue a series of directives designed to correct the worst abuses in the treatment of foreign volunteers). The Freiwilligen Legion *Flandern* was sent to the northern sector of the Eastern Front in early 1942, where it suffered heavy losses. Tollenaere fell in action, and subsequently became the Horst Wessel of the VNV.

RIGHT: Flemish Feld Post stamps. The western European SS legions were supported in a minor sense by the sale of so-called legion postage stamps. These fell into two general types: volunteer legion stamps that were bought by individual members of the legion, as well as family and friends, which were used with regular stamps. They had no fiscal value, but were designed to show patriotism and loyalty. The other type were stamps produced in the country in which that nation's legion had been formed; these stamps had an official value.

LEFT: Belgium also issued a set of stamps in honour of the Walloons while they were an army unit. As can be seen, they bear two prices. The first number is the actual cost of the stamp, while the second constitutes a surcharge for charity, in this case for the Walloon legionnaires. The authorisation for national legions came from Hitler a few days after the invasion of the Soviet Union, to take part in the 'battle against Bolshevism'. At this time Himmler was only interested in what he called 'Germanic' legions, composed of Norwegians, Netherlanders, Swedes, Danes and Flemings. Before the first legions were despatched to the Eastern Front, Himmler laid down the status of these units: the legionnaires were placed under German military law and SS regulations, they were given SS rank equivalent to that previously held in their national army, they were not made German citizens but were bound by personal oath to Hitler, and they would receive SS pay and compensation for dependents. Their uniform was SS, with a national emblem in place of SS runes. The legion concept was eventually to break down due to bad handling by SS training centres, subsequent disillusionment among recruits and heavy losses on the Eastern Front. But the flow of western European recruits into the Waffen-SS continued. The final count was as follows: 50,000 Dutch, 40,000 Belgians (Flemings and Walloons), 20,000 French, 6000 Danes, 6000 Norwegians and 1200 from Switzerland, Sweden and Luxembourg. These recruits were the best of the Waffen-SS's foreign volunteers by far, and were to form one of the élite SS divisions: the 5th SS Panzer Division *Wiking*.

FOR VALOUR

Awards for Germans and foreign volunteers proliferated as the war progressed. They were not won easily, and their recipients were justly proud of their achievements.

LEFT: Golden Hitler Youth Honour Badge with Oak-leaves. Awarded for exceptional service in or to the Hitler Youth, no more than 250 were awarded. It could be awarded to Hitler Youth members, Germans who were not members of the Hitler Youth, and could be conferred upon foreign nationals.

ABOVE: Tollenaere Commemorative Badge, which was instituted to commemorate the death of Reimond Tollenaere, the leader of the Flemish 'Black Brigade'. He met a 'hero's death' at Kopzy near Leningrad on 22 January 1942. Subsequently the VNV leadership instituted the badge in his memory as a reward for loyalty and sacrifice. It was usually worn on the left-pocket of the military uniform.

LEFT: Military Training In Germany Badge for Italian personnel, an award instituted to recognise those Italians who underwent military training in Germany. These men were mainly absorbed into the Waffen-SS or affiliated units. The exact criteria for the award are unknown, but is believed that it was for three months' instruction and was for young volunteers who successfully completed their advanced military training.

ABOVE: Germanic SS proficiency runes bronze and silver. Most of the Germanic SS formations possessed sports badges of their own, but on 15 August 1943 Himmler introduced this award, its requirements being the same for all nationalities in the Waffen-SS. The tests leading to the award were divided into three sections: individual athletic tests, team or group tests, and individual political knowledge examinations.

LEFT: SS-Standartenführer der Reserve Léon Degrelle, Knight's Cross at his neck, takes the salute at the parade of the Sturmbrigade *Wallonie* on its return to Belgium after its heroics in the Cherkassy Pocket in early 1944. Note he wears the Badge of Honour of Rex on his left-breast pocket. A popular figure among his men, he was also admired for his leadership and valour by Hitler, who said: 'If I had a son, I would wish him to be like you.' Fighting the Russians until the end of the war, he escaped to Norway and then Spain, where he died on 31 March 1994.

BELOW: Front Line Soldiers Badge, which was instituted in October 1943 by Vidkum Quisling, leader of the Norwegian fascists, and awarded to all Norwegian military personnel who saw active service on the Eastern Front. It was worn on the left-breast pocket of the military uniform. Women as well as men were eligible for the award. There is photographic evidence of an Anne Gunhild Moxanes of the *Wiking* Division wearing the Front Line Soldiers Badge (she was also awarded the Iron Cross Second Class). Interestingly, a similar badge exists with the inscription 'Front Sister', which has a nurse standing over a wounded man.

ABOVE: The Badge of Honour of Rex, sometimes referred to as the Rexist 'Blood Order' (Belgian's fascist party). It was awarded in four types – Bronze, Silver, Gold and a form of the Gold with Diamonds – for service as members of the Rexist Party (Bronze), and as a reward for persons not members of Degrelle's party for service to the party (Silver). The criteria for the Gold class is unknown. The Gold with Diamonds type was awarded to Victor Matthys, deputy party leader, on 8 August 1944. From 16 October 1944 it could be worn on SS attire.

CHAPTER ELEVEN

High Tide in the East
The Waffen-SS at Kharkov and Kursk

The German defeat at Stalingrad precipitated a general crisis for the Wehrmacht in southern Russia. The task of reversing this dire situation was assigned to the newly created I SS Panzer Corps, commanded by SS-Obergruppenführer Paul 'Papa' Hausser.

The corps deployed in the area between Volokomovka on the River Oskol and Kupiansk on the River Donetz. During the first week of February 1943, the Waffen-SS repulsed a number of Russian attacks which cost the Red Army dear. It was apparent that the Red Army's goal was Kharkov, to be taken by an enormous pincer movement, whose southern claw had to push through the ground held by the *Leibstandarte* Division and the army's 320th Infantry Division, while the northern claw was to smash through the region northeast of Belgorod.

LEFT: A Soviet tank knocked out by II SS Panzer Corps at the Battle of Kursk July 1943.

OPPOSITE: German assault guns being moved to the front for the Kursk Offensive. Hitler regarded victory at Kursk as being vital to convince the German people and his allies that neither he nor his Third Reich were finished.

KHARKOV IS LOST

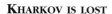

On 9 February, during blizzard conditions, the *Das Reich* Division began a slow withdrawal westwards to a new defensive line on the Donetz. However, Soviet pressure forced it to withdraw to the east of Kharkov. In the north, meanwhile, the Germans were being forced back towards the city, which was slowly being surrounded. Due to mounting pressure in the south, the Germans had to relinquish Zmiyov to the Soviets. The only German defences outside Kharkov now consisted of scattered strongholds.

True to form, Hitler ordered that Kharkov was to be held at all costs. SS-Obergruppenführer 'Papa' Hausser received the order in the city, but realised it was futile to try to hold a doomed city. He ordered the destruction of all military installations to prevent them falling into Soviet hands when Kharkov eventually fell. Its suburbs were penetrated on 14 February, with I SS Panzer Corps' rear area being infiltrated during the next 24 hours. The Soviet advance was temporarily stemmed to the northwest of Kharkov by a counterattack launched by elements of *Das Reich*, but on 15 February Hausser again sort permission to pull out of the city. Later that day he was informed to stay put, an order he chose to ignore. He then instructed I SS Panzer Corps to evacuate Kharkov.

THE FÜHRER'S FURY DEMANDS VICTORY

In a rage Hitler flew instantly to Army Group South's headquarters at Zaporozhye and ordered that Kharkov be retaken. The Soviets could easily be ejected, he raged, and an immediate counterattack should be launched, with I SS Panzer Corps in the van. Field Marshal von Manstein, one of Germany's finest military leaders, had other plans, though, the objective of which was no less than the encirclement and annihilation of the Soviet armies that were moving towards the River Dnieper. I SS Panzer Corps was to be deployed as the upper claw in a large pincer movement, while the lower claw would be formed by the army's 4th Panzer Army under the command of General Hermann Hoth. Hitler was unimpressed by Manstein's scheme, but his own plans were thwarted by the *Totenkopf* Division becoming completely bogged down in the mud. He therefore begrudgingly approved Manstein's alternative plan.

LEFT: The smiling face of the Waffen-SS in the spring of 1943. Himmler's troops had much to smile about, for after their victory at Kharkov they were high in Hitler's esteem, and were being supplied with the best tanks, assault guns and equipment for the forthcoming summer offensive.

Division. The victory at Kharkov was complete, but at a monumental price: over 11,500 killed.

Though the front had now been stabilised, the Red Army still controlled a huge salient around the city of Kursk that bulged into German territory. Hitler became obsessed by this salient, and soon preparations were under way to eradicate it. Militarily this made sense, as across its base the bulge measured a mere 160km (100 miles). Victory would regain the German initiative on the Eastern Front, and release a great number of troops to counter the anticipated Allied invasion of southern Europe. It would have the added advantage of destroying up to 15 Soviet armies if the offensive was successful. Unfortunately, what was obvious to German planners was also crystal clear to their enemies, and the Red Army began to construct massive defences in the Kursk salient.

HITLER'S PLAN AT KURSK

Field Marshal Erich von Manstein and General Heinz Guderian suggested that the Soviets be allowed to take the offensive, with the Germans withdrawing gradually, resulting in the Red Army over-extending itself. It could then be hit with full force – the Kharkov scenario repeated. Hitler was unimpressed by their plan, and ordered his offensive to be planned for and undertaken with all speed. It was code-named 'Zitadelle', or Operation 'Citadel'. The main blows at the Soviet forces were to be struck from south of Orel by the 9th Army of Army Group Centre, and from north of Kharkov by the 9th Panzer Army and Panzer Group *Kempf* from Army Group South. By striking in the general direction of Kursk, the German High Command reckoned to surround and destroy the forces of the Central and Voronezh Fronts defending the salient, to straighten the frontline, and in the event of success to develop its offensive into the rear of the southwest front – plan 'Panther'. There was also the possibility of a subsequent strike to the northeast to outflank Moscow, and come out behind all Soviet forces in the centre of the front.

II SS Panzer corps, commanded by SS-Obergruppenführer Paul 'Papa' Hausser, was part of the 4th Panzer Army. It comprised the 1st SS Panzer Division *Leibstandarte*, 2nd SS Panzer Division *Das Reich* and 3rd SS Panzer Division *Totenkopf*. The German Army fielded 900,000 men, 10,000 artillery field pieces and 2700 tanks, and air cover would be supplied by around 2000 Luftwaffe aircraft. But it would be the Waffen-SS that would play a disproportionately large part in the greatest armoured clash in history.

The German attack caught the exhausted Soviets completely unawares, and I SS Panzer Corps and the 4th Panzer Army joined forces on 4 March to begin the assault on the city. The original plan stated Kharkov should be taken by a three-pronged assault: the *Totenkopf* Division was to attack from the northwest, the north of the city was saved for the *Leibstandarte* Division, and *Das Reich* was to drive around to the north and attack Smiyev down the eastern side. Scrapping this move, an attack from the west was now the new objective of the *Das Reich* Division, and it penetrated the outskirts of the city against stiffening resistance.

I SS PANZER CORPS RETAKES KHARKOV

To the north, pushing down the main Belgorod-Kharkov road, the *Leibstandarte*'s SS-Panzergrenadier Regiment 1, under the command of SS-Standartenführer Fritz Witt, smashed its way into Kharkov. On Witt's right was SS-Panzergrenadier Regiment 2 under SS-Standartenführer Theodor 'Teddi' Wisch. On the left flank was SS-Obersturmbannführer Kurt Meyer and his reconnaissance battalion. The Russians inside Kharkov were trapped, though they tried desperately to fight their way through the German lines.

The *Totenkopf*'s panzers confronted Soviet units on the Kharkov-Belgorod road and destroyed them, swung around the north of the city and then southeast to Tshuguyev, where they captured the Donetz crossing. During the next few days the *Totenkopf* Division had to repulse Soviet units fleeing from Kharkov, as well as having to cope with counterattacks from fresh Red Army formations to the east. These actions resulted in the annihilation of the Soviet 25th Guards Rifle

The Battle of Kursk began on 5 July, and the Germans soon discovered the scale of the defences they were up against, as artillery and mortar fire rained down on them. The German troops tried to conceal themselves in the tall grass, but found the fields had been sowed with anti-personnel mines. In addition, the Red Army Air Force mounted effective attacks, despite the Luftwaffe having air superiority over the area, inflicting heavy casualties on both men and equipment.

II SS PANZER CORPS ATTACKS

In the south the *Totenkopf* Division smashed into the Soviet 52nd Guards Division, which after tenacious combat was overcome. More Soviet defence lines were attacked by the *Totenkopf* Division on 9 July, and under the savage Waffen-SS onslaught the defences began to crumble. The extent of the advance was now causing deep concern to the Soviet commanders, who decided it was time to commit the 5th Guards Tank Army and two tank brigades from the reserve to crush the armoured spearhead.

On 5 July the *Leibstandarte*, positioned to the south of the *Totenkopf* Division, had also enjoyed initial success. The Russians' first line of defences were penetrated, though progress then began to slow due to Soviet resistance. In addition, by the end of the third day tank losses were affecting II SS Panzer Corps. Some 160 Panthers, for example, had been lost from an initial total of 200. There were also problems with the Ferdinand assault guns, which had, through a design oversight, not been equipped with a machine gun for close-quarters combat, leaving it defenceless in these situations.

The *Totenkopf* Division, leading II SS Panzer Corps, continued its drive northwards, and to the west of Prokhorovka the Soviet forces were pushed aside. The 5th Guards Tank Army, the main reserve of the Soviets, was getting ready to spring its own offensive, though, its objective being to stop II SS Panzer Corps. The Russian preparations were rudely interrupted with the appearance of Hausser's command, which swung smartly eastwards, the *Totenkopf* Division taking the left flank, the *Leibstandarte* the centre and *Das Reich* the right flank.

The Germans were held to the west of Prokhorovka – just. But the Russians still had a problem: if they waited for all their units to arrive the Germans would also have time to acquire reinforcements (III Panzer Corps was driving northwards along Hausser's right flank with its 300 tanks). A two-part plan was therefore implemented: a force of two mechanised brigades, a mechanised guards corps, an armoured brigade and a guards rifle division was sent to

intercept III Panzer corps. The remaining force would undertake an immediate attack against II SS Panzer Corps. With the advantage of the sun at their backs, the Soviets broke cover and drove at full speed straight at the amazed Germans. A battle developed at virtually point-blank range, which favoured the Soviet T-34's lighter 76mm gun.

The *Totenkopf* Division, positioned on II SS-Panzer Corps' left flank, was engaged by XXXI Guards Corps and XXIII Guards Corps, which halted the *Totenkopf*'s advance and forced it onto the defensive. Meanwhile, II Guard Tank Corps was meting out stiff opposition to the *Das Reich* Division. The high point of the battle at Prokhorovka was reached during the afternoon, with the outcome hanging by a thread. Decisively, the Soviet blocking force had halted III Panzer Corps as it battled towards II SS Panzer Corps.

By nightfall, with both sides utterly exhausted, the battle was reduced to a few small individual skirmishes. That day 300 German tanks had been destroyed. Hitler decided to suspend Operation 'Citadel' on 13 July officially, albeit the fighting continued until 15 July. The final nail in the Kursk Offensive's coffin was Hitler's order that the *Leibstandarte*, *Das Reich* and *Totenkopf* Divisions be withdrawn from the Eastern Front. The Allied invasion of Sicily had taken place on 10 July, and Hitler believed the strengthening of the Italian Front could only be achieved by his élite Waffen-SS divisions. At Kursk all the offensive's territorial gains had been lost by 23 July. The battle had inflicted resounding losses on both sides, losses the Germans were never to recover from. The losses were catastrophic in both men and armoured fighting vehicles. The Eastern Front now was to drain the German forces through attrition, while for the Soviets the battle marked the turning point of their war.

RIGHT: By mid-1943 the Germans were on the defensive everywhere, but in the East Hitler was convinced he could wrest the initiative away from the enemy. To do so he looked to his loyal and aggressive Waffen-SS divisions.

BELOW: StuG III assault gun of the *Leibstandarte* Division in action in Russia at the beginning of February 1943. Hitler ordered the newly formed I SS Panzer Corps to the Eastern Front in January. The Soviet winter offensive of 1942 had torn massive holes in the German frontline in southern Russia, and it was the job of I SS Panzer to plug the gaps. The Waffen-SS soldiers did not fail, as thousands of Italian, Hungarian and German soldiers streamed west in disarray. The Russians, expecting an easy victory, were shocked when they ran into strong SS units, and received bloody noses in the process. The thinly spread *Leibstandarte* in particular held the vital bridgehead at Pechenege against everything the Red Army could throw against it.

RIGHT: Well-wrapped Waffen-SS soldiers in southern Russia in February 1943. The German disaster at Stalingrad had created a crisis for the Third Reich on the Eastern Front: the second half of January had witnessed the Red Army tearing a 320km (200-mile) gap in the German front between the city of Voronezh and the great bend in the River Don. Into this gap flowed huge Soviet tank and infantry armies. Stalin sensed victory on the Eastern Front, but I SS Panzer Corps was to dictate otherwise. Hausser's corps was immensely powerful. The *Totenkopf* Division, for example, required 120 trains to transport its men and vehicles across Europe to the rail yards at Kiev, the main terminus for German reinforcements sent to southern Russia.

LEFT: A Waffen-SS grenadier chalks up another Soviet tank knocked out in southern Russia. By the beginning of February it was apparent that Kharkov was in danger of being encircled by the Red Army. The divisions of I SS Panzer Corps were slowly forced to retire into the city. On 9 February, for example, the *Das Reich* Division pulled back from the perimeter it held along the River Donetz, its troops retreating in a blizzard and in waist-high snow, all the time fighting off Russian attacks.

BELOW: Tanks of I SS Panzer Corps near Kharkov, early 1943. The élite Waffen-SS formations were officially designated panzergrenadier divisions, i.e. partially armoured, motorised infantry divisions. However, the élite SS divisions had long been equipped with tanks. Indeed, in December 1942, when Germany's inventory of the new Tiger and Panther tanks totalled 74, two companies of Tigers went to the *Leibstandarte* Division. The élite SS formations were thus panzer divisions.

ABOVE: Machine-embroidered BeVo pattern enlisted cuff band introduced in March 1943 for wear by members of the 3rd SS-Totenkopf Grenadier Regiment. On 26 February 1943, SS-Obergruppenführer Theodor Eicke was on an inspection flight on the Eastern Front when his light aircraft was shot down, crashing behind enemy lines and killing him. His body was rescued by members of the *Totenkopf* Division and then given a Viking-style funeral at a divisional cemetery near Orelka, Russia. By order of Hitler dated 2 March 1943, the honorary title 'Theodor Eicke' was created, which was conferred upon the 3rd SS-Totenkopf Grenadier Regiment. The regiment later became SS-Panzergrenadier Regiment 6 *Theodor Eicke*.

BELOW: SS-Obergruppenführer und General der Waffen-SS Theodor Eicke, killed in action on 26 February 1943. The creator and leader of the *Totenkopf* Division had few friends among the army, even the Nazi hierarchy, but to his men was an inspired commander who shared their hardships. The division was very much made in his own image. and during the war displayed those qualities he admired most: fanatical determination and utter ruthlessness. It is no exaggeration to say that Eicke elicited a semi-religious devotion from his men.

RIGHT: Formal award casement for the Knight's Cross of the Iron Cross with Oakleaves document. Early recipients received the large leather folder that was padded on the front binding, with a gold metal national emblem adorning it. The inside of the cover was white, and on the rear inner edge was the name of the artist in gold: Frieda Thiersch.

LEFT: The formal document for the Knight's Cross presented to SS-Obergruppenführer Theodor Eicke. This was posthumously awarded to him in recognition of his division's achievement on the Eastern Front. The *Totenkopf* itself was so highly rated by the Russians that the Soviet authorities promised a bounty for every captured *Totenkopf* Division cuff band. When the general German retreat began on the Eastern Front following the defeat at Kursk, officers from the *Totenkopf*'s divisional staff, assisted by a small number of selected soldiers, exhumed Eicke's body and transported it by lorry to Kiev to prevent it falling into the hands of the Red Army.

RIGHT: An honour guard flanks the memorial to those of the Belgian Nazi Vlaamsch Nationaal Verbond (VNV) who had been killed fighting the Russians. The Freiwilligen Legion *Flandern*, composed of Flemish Belgians, suffered crippling losses on the Eastern Front in March 1942. In one week of fighting alone, for example, the unit lost over 1000 men, and ended up with a strength of only 60 soldiers. The shattered survivors were withdrawn from the front to Debica in Poland in May 1943, where what was left of the legion was disbanded.

KHARKOV

I SS Panzer Corps' victory at Kharkov in March 1943 was a brilliant stroke by Manstein, and convinced Hitler that the Waffen-SS held the key to victory on the Eastern Front.

ABOVE: SS panzers move out for Manstein's counterattack that will retake Kharkov. The Red Army, flushed with success at wresting the city from the fascist invader, was taken completely by surprise by the German attack. XLVIII Panzer Corps pushed towards the River Samara, and Red Army units fled northwards in near panic. German morale soared. On 22 February 1943, the *Das Reich* Division raced towards Pavlograd supported by Stuka dive-bombers. It then linked up with the *Totenkopf* Division and the two formations drove parallel to retreating Russian forces. The demoralised Red Army units were all but slaughtered during the following few days, two of Stalin's armies being destroyed. On the frozen wastes lay around 600 destroyed T-34 tanks (enough tanks were captured to equip an entire panzer regiment for the *Das Reich* Division), plus another 600 anti-tank guns and 400 artillery pieces. In desperation the Soviets pumped more forces into the area

south of Kharkov. However, Hausser laid a trap for these units, and they were soon being pushed towards the entrenched *Leibstandarte* by the *Das Reich* and *Totenkopf* Divisions. The Russians were annihilated, and the gates of Kharkov now lay open to the Germans. On 4 March 1943 I SS Panzer Corps and the 4th Panzer Army joined forces to begin the final assault on the city. A grenadier of the *Deutschland* Regiment, *Das Reich* Division, provides an insight into fighting at this time: 'Visibility down to 1000 metres. The men have packed the ammunition boxes, the machine guns and heavy weapons, such as mortars, on to sledges shaped like kayaks. The gunners of the flak company check the ammo belts once again. The mine-laying teams are probing with bayonets because the batteries for their detectors have long since gone flat. The men kneel on the ground sifting through the snow and then digging out the frozen mines with bayonets.'

RIGHT: SS-Standartenführer Fritz Witt (smoking cigar) of the *Leibstandarte* Division in Kharkov in March 1943. Witt's SS-Panzergrenadier Regiment 1 had battled its way into the city and had captured the psychologically important Red Square. The fighting was savage, with the Waffen-SS soldiers engaging in house-to-house fighting, often room-to-room fighting, which carried on for three days. Those Red Army units trapped in the city desperately tried to break out of the city to the north – but to no avail.

BELOW: The Waffen-SS in Kharkov. The *Das Reich* Division penetrated the city's western side on 12 March, and reached the main railway station. Meanwhile, SS-Obersturmbannführer Kurt Meyer and his reconnaissance detachment linked up with another of the *Leibstandarte*'s units, SS-Sturmbannführer Joachim Peiper's panzergrenadier battalion. Together they smashed into the east and southeastern sectors of the city to flush out what remained of the Russians. Late in the afternoon of 15 March, the last Russian resistance in the city's tractor factory had ceased. The city of Kharkov had been retaken. Peiper was then sent northwards to reach the Donetz, which he did on 18 March, linking up with the army's élite *Grossdeutschland* Division. Manstein's four-week counteroffensive was over, and the Wehrmacht once again stood on the ground which it had conquered in 1942. The reputation of the Waffen-SS, among friend and foe alike, soared.

ABOVE: One of the Wehrmacht's Tiger tanks in Russia in 1943. Well-protected and armed with the formidable 8.8cm anti-aircraft gun, it was ideally suited to the defensive role of the panzer force from 1943 onwards. After Kharkov a period of calm descended on the Eastern Front, which gave the exhausted Germans time to recover. Most of Hitler's generals were of the opinion that offensive operations could only be renewed in 1944 at the earliest, as Manstein stated: 'The question now was how the German side should continue the struggle the following summer. Obviously, after so many major formations had been lost, there would no longer be the forces available to mount another crucial offensive on the scale of 1941 and 1942.' However, the success of the SS at Kharkov convinced Hitler that he could regain the initiative in 1943.

RIGHT: *Totenkopf* Tigers just prior to the Kursk Offensive. For the attempt to crush the Kursk salient, II SS Panzer Corps, comprising the *Leibstandarte*, *Das Reich* and *Totenkopf* Divisions, had over 340 tanks and 195 self-propelled guns. Each Waffen-SS division had its own Tiger unit. Its task, as part of Colonel-General Hoth's 4th Panzer Army, was to be the armoured spearhead of the assault to eliminate the Soviet reserves. But in the salient itself were 1,300,000 Russian troops and 3300 tanks.

LEFT: A Panzer Mk V Panther, Germany's new medium tank for the Kursk Offensive. Armed with a 7.5cm gun, its sloped armour gave it good protection against anti-tank rounds. The Panther and the Tiger gave the German panzer force a qualitative superiority over its enemies for the first time since 1939, which in the hands of experienced crews would go a long way to offset the Wehrmacht's numerical inferiority. Unfortunately, at Kursk the Panther suffered teething problems, such as catching fire!

BELOW: One of the many assault guns possessed by the German Army at Kursk. The tactics II SS Panzer Corps employed for breaking through the dense Russian defences around the salient consisted of the Panzerkeil (armoured wedge). This was made up of Tigers flanked by Panthers, while the Panthers themselves were flanked by Panzer IIIs, IVs and StuG III assault guns. The armoured wedge was a fearsome sight on the battlefield, but at Kursk it suffered from two main weaknesses: the unreliability of the Panther and the slow speed of the Tiger. On the other hand, the terrain of the battlefield was conducive to armoured warfare, being a huge plain covered either with corn or by belts of tall steppe grass. Unfortunately the sand roads turned to mud when it rained, and the Russians had the tactical advantage as the plain rose gently towards Kursk, giving them complete observation. They also had the densest defences the world had ever seen.

KURSK

On 5 July 1943 the clash at Kursk began. Nearly one million German soldiers tried to cut through six Soviet defence lines, an attack which became a battle of attrition.

BELOW: Members of II SS Panzer Corps hitch a ride on Panzer IIIs during the Battle of Kursk. Hausser's troops began the battle at 0400 hours on 5 July, passing easily through the first belt of Russian mines, which had been dealt with by SS engineers. The Waffen-SS penetrated 19km (12 miles) into the salient on the first day. Red Army tanks and guns were destroyed (a certain Michael Wittmann knocking out eight enemy tanks on the first day), but Russian resistance started to stiffen and losses began to rise. The *Leibstandarte* alone lost 97 killed on the first day.

RIGHT: SS-Untersturmführer Walter Otto, a tank commander at Kursk. The leadership of Waffen-SS junior commanders during the battle was exemplary. SS-Unterscharführer Kurt Sametreiter, for example, platoon leader in the *Leibstandarte*'s tank-destroyer battalion, knocked out 24 Russian tanks near the village of Stalinsk with his four anti-tank guns. He and his men then repulsed an infantry attack. For this he was awarded the Knight's Cross. But II SS Panzer Corps was still losing men: by the second day the *Leibstandarte* had lost 181 killed.

LEFT: Waffen-SS grenadiers wait for an artillery barrage to lift before continuing the advance at Kursk. By 12 July Hausser's corps was west of Prokhorovka, where it met the Soviet 5th Guards Tank Army in the greatest armoured clash in history. In the ensuing days the Germans lost over 300 tanks, whereas the Russians lost around half their tanks.

BELOW: A.Tiger engages targets at Kursk. Many Waffen-SS Tigers enjoyed high kill rates during the battle. The Tiger-equipped No 13 Company, 1st SS Panzer Regiment, *Leibstandarte* Division, for example, knocked out 20 Russian T-34s during a two-hour battle on 7 July, and the division claimed 500 tanks destroyed up to 14 July.

BELOW: The failure to break through at Prokhorovka effectively ended the Kursk Offensive. Hitler suspended 'Citadel' on 13 July, bringing an end his operation that had cost 100,000 German dead. The Russians had lost far more – 250,000 killed, 600,000 wounded and half their entire tank force – but their losses could be made good. II SS Panzer Corps was in a desperate state, possessing only 183 tanks and 64 self-propelled guns. As Guderian stated: ' The armoured formations, reformed and re-equipped with much effort, had lost heavily both in men and equipment.'

CHAPTER TWELVE

Italian Adventure
Fighting the Allies and partisans in Italy

By 1943 Hitler was concerned about Mussolini's regime crumbling, fears that were reinforced in June when he was compelled to resign from the Fascist Grand Council, and in July when the Allies invaded Sicily. In addition, bands of partisans were forming against the Germans and Italian fascists. In Hitler's opinion only his élite Waffen-SS divisions could strengthen the Italian Front. In the last week of July 1943, the Führer's fears concerning Italy were confirmed when, on 25 July, the king dismissed Mussolini.

LEFT: A machine-gunner of the 24th SS Gebirgs Division *Karstjäger* opens fire on a partisan position in northern Italy. Note the observer scanning the horizon.

OPPOSITE: Mixed Waffen-SS and German Army troops in Italy in late 1943. The heavy tank in the background is a PzKpfw VI Tiger, Ausf B, King Tiger.

THE SS RESCUES MUSSOLINI
The new government under Marshal Badoglio lasted six weeks, before being supplanted by a German military regime. Hitler immediately began plans to rescue *Il Duce* and strengthen the German hold on Italy. His initial idea was to transfer II SS Panzer Corps from Army Group South to Italy, though in the event only the corps headquarters and the *Leibstandarte* Division, minus some of its tanks, were transferred from the Eastern Front in July 1943.

On the afternoon of 12 September 1943, gliders carrying a force of German shock troops under SS-Hauptsturmführer Otto Skorzeny rescued Mussolini from his imprisonment in the Gran Sasso Hotel. After a hasty meeting with Hitler Mussolini returned to Italy to set up his new Republican Fascist Government in Northern Italy, but it was too little, too late. In October, Mussolini was obliged by the Germans to withdraw from Romagna to Lake Garda. He appointed Marshal Graziani as his Minister of Defence, but the reality was that the German Army, with its headquarters at Belluno, was now an occupational force. At first the Commander-in-Chief was Field Marshal Erwin Rommel, then Field Marshal

Albert Kesselring from November 1943. The German Ambassador, Rudolf Rahn, represented Ribbentrop and the Foreign Office, and there was a whole network of SS officials with thousands of SS troops of differing nationalities: Volksdeutsche, Czechs, Slovaks and Ukrainians. SS-Obergruppenführer und General der Polizei Dr Ernst Kaltenbrunner, as the head of the Reich Sicherheitshauptamt, was represented by Wilhelm Harster, and Himmler was represented by SS-Obergruppenführer Karl Wolff and SS-Standartenführer Dr Eugen Dollman.

SAVAGE REPRISALS
In July 1943, Wolff set up an advanced staff in Munich to prepare an operational SS and police command in Italy in the event of the possible defection of Badoglio. Wolff's responsibilities included the suppression of the partisans. This was far from easy, especially after June 1944 when the Allies took Rome, the Germans falling back to the Gothic Line. Predictably German reprisals against partisan actions were harsh. Units of the *Leibstandarte* Division, for example, during their stay in northern Italy, played a leading role in the murder of the inhabitants and the destruction of the town of Boves in September 1943. This action was billed as an SS operation against anti-fascist partisans. The *Leibstandarte* Division took part in the disarming of Italian Army units after

LEFT: A Waffen-SS 5cm Pak 38 anti-tank gun hidden in an orchard in northern Italy. The crew are being briefed by the battery commander, no doubt about the coming Allied armoured assault. The Pak 38, which entered service in 1940, was a good weapon, with good mobility, lightness and a low silhouette.

Marshal Graziani, Mussolini's Minister of Defence, addressed the legionnaires of the division. The 2nd Battalion was awarded a regimental pennant carrying the word 'Vendetta'. Also in action at Anzio was the SS Füsilier Bataillon *Debica*, which also suffered heavy casualties. These units were the first to be accorded the honour of removing their red collar patches and replacing them with those of the Waffen-SS.

the overthrow of Mussolini's regime in September 1943, before returning to the Eastern Front in the autumn.

The major Waffen-SS unit to serve in Italy was the élite *Leibstandarte* Division, but in the summer of 1943 a new Waffen-SS panzergrenadier division, *Reichsführer-SS*, was formed. In addition, there were a number of Waffen-SS units that had been constructed out of the indigenous Italian population, and these were employed in the fierce anti-partisan fighting that was erupting on the Adriatic coast. These units were also deployed against the Allies at Anzio.

ITALIAN SS UNITS

The first moves to form an 'Italian Legion' emanated from Major Fortunato, a Bersaglieri officer of the former Italian Expeditionary Corps in Russia. By the end of 1943, at the training camp at Münsingen in the Black Forest area of southern Germany, the Germans had succeeded in assembling about 15,000 pro-Mussolini Italians. From these they formed an assault brigade known as the *Prima Brigata d'Assalto della Legione SS Italiana* (the 1st Assault Brigade of the Italian SS Legion). In Germany it was refered to as the 1st Sturmbrigade Italienische Freiwilligen Legion. In January 1944, the brigade was dispatched to Italy and was engaged in some minor actions against the partisans. It first experienced full-scale combat when it was committed to battle at the Anzio beachhead in May 1944,;it was raised to divisional strength in September 1944 and accorded the divisional number 29. The Italians now became the 29th Waffen-Grenadier Division der SS (Italienishe Nr 1). The 2nd Battalion of the 1st Regiment suffered severe losses in the three week battle at Anzio, losing 340 men from its compliment of 650. On 23 November 1944, at Mariano Comense,

THE *KARSTJÄGER* DIVISION

The 24th SS Gebirgs Division *Karstjäger* was another Italian division, though made up of pro-fascist Italian and German Volksdeutsche personnel. It was formed around a special anti-partisan mountain combat company, the SS Karstwehr Kompanie. This had been raised in the summer of 1942 to fight Tito's partisans in the Carso (Karst) and Julian Alps. After the fall of Mussolini, Himmler decided that the Karstwehr Battalion should be augmented by locally recruited Volksdeutsche from the South Tyrol and latterly by Italian fascist 'loyalists'. The division consisted of two mountain infantry regiments and one mountain artillery regiment, and at Moggio in the Italian province of Udine a divisional headquarters was established. Almost all the actions fought by this unit were against the partisans, except for one very brief skirmish in the latter stages of the war with the British.

The origins of the 16th SS Panzergrenadier Division *Reichsführer-SS* can be traced back to the escort battalion named Begleit-Bataillon *Reichsführer-SS* that had been created on 15 May 1941, within Himmler's Headquarters Staff (Kommandostab RFSS). In February 1943, Hitler had ordered that this escort battalion, having proved itself in battle, be upgraded to the status of an assault brigade. Thus SS-Sturmbrigade *Reichsführer-SS* was formed, and in the summer of 1943 was stationed on the island of Corsica. It was transferred to the Italian mainland in October 1943 when the Allies took the islands of Sardinia and Corsica.

Reichsführer-SS was built around a cadre of personnel from SS-Sturmbrigade *Reichsführer-SS*, and the commander of the new division was a former regimental commander in the *Totenkopf* Division, SS-Brigadeführer Max Simon. During November 1943 the divisional elements were raised around the SS-Sturmbrigade *Reichsführer-SS*. The division was still being trained when the Allies established the Anzio bridgehead in January 1944. Elements of the division had to be quickly rushed to the front, where they remained in combat in the Anzio/Nettuno bridgehead until 9 March 1944. In early March, in addition to the divisional elements detached and fighting south of Rome, there were others stationed in Italy. The 6th and 14th Companies of SS-Panzergrenadier Regiment 35, for example, were based at Mussolini's headquarters at Lake Garda.

REICHSFÜHRER-SS IN HUNGARY

Concerns about the possibility of Hitler's Hungarian allies abandoning the Axis and joining the Russians prompted the Führer to launch Operation 'Margarethe'. When this took place most of the remaining elements of the *Reichsführer-SS* Division were transferred to Hungary to seize power from Admiral Horthy's regime. It was a strengthened but nonetheless incomplete division that set off in March 1944 through Baden in Austria for Hungary. It took up positions as an occupational force around Debrecen. In April, the detached elements returned from Italy and the division was complete for the first time. The Hungarian problem was not resolved by any means, but the Allies' advance into northern Italy was cause for grave concern and it was decided to transfer the division to Italy to try and hold the British 8th Army. The formation was transported southwards from Parma to Grosseto, on the west coast facing the island of Elba. The British drove the division back past Siena to Pisa, and by August it had been driven back as far north as Carrara. The division fought defensively, first around Carrara in August, and then retiring in a north-

easterly direction towards Bologna across the Appennino Tosco-Emiliano Mountains for the remainder of 1944. Elements of the division, with SS-Sturmbannführer Walter Reder's armoured reconnaissance unit taking a leading role, were forced to ward off countless attacks by the partisans. On 12 August 1944, Reder's unit undertook an action against the *Garibaldi* Brigade, moving on its base in the village of Santa'Anna di Stazzema in Versilia. The neighbouring village of Farnocchia was reportedly set on fire by the SS troops, before they moved on to burn Santa'Anna to the ground and kill a number of people. In a later operation at Padule di Fucecchio, the same unit is reported to have murdered a further 120 civilians. In the last days of September 1944, Reder and his men descended on the Marzabotto area and killed a large number of partisans. Whether civilians were deliberately killed or just got in the way is a matter of speculation.

In October 1944, command of the division passed to another former *Totenkopf* Division regimental commander, SS-Oberführer Otto Baum. The *Reichsfüher-SS* Division was located in the northeast of Italy in January 1945, and it came down from its rocky positions in the Appenines in early February to continue its withdrawal. It continued northeastwards, crossing the Via Emilia, southeast of Bologna, and taking up positions again, this time southwest of the Valli di Comacchio Lake. These positions were encompassed in a triangular area that had its corners delineated by the towns of Alfonsine, Fusigano and Lavezzola. In a ruse to confuse the Allies, the division was withdrawn from Italy in disguise. To have let the Allies into the secret that the Italian Front had been so effectively undermined and was crumbling would have done the German military cause irreparable damage. The division's time in Italy was at an end. Like many SS units, it had left a legacy of hatred behind it.

RIGHT: Having left behind its heavy weapons in Russia, in Italy the Waffen-SS had to use anything that came to hand. These SS soldiers are manning a 3.7cm Pak 35/36 anti-tank gun, nicknamed the 'door knocker' due to its inability to penetrate the armour of Allied tanks. By 1941 it was obsolete.

RIGHT: These troops are probably members of the 16th SS Panzergrenadier Division *Reichsführer-SS* conducting anti-partisan sweeps in northern Italy. By late 1943 the partisans were becoming a thorn in the side of the Germans. Bands of young men increasingly took to the mountains to form partisan bands, and they were often assisted by local peasants. The mountains gave perfect cover to the guerrillas, from where they launched attacks against both German and Italian fascist formations.

BELOW: The Germans pull out of northern Italy. The Waffen-SS did not play a major role in the Italian campaign, but it left its mark on the Italian people. SS-Obersturmbannführer Herbert Kappler, for example, had 335 civilian hostages shot in reprisal for the killing by partisans of policemen in Rome on 23 March 1944. The hostages were killed by shots to the head.

ABOVE: Members of the *Leibstandarte* Division in Italy in late 1943. Earlier, in September 1943, troops from the division had played a leading part in the murder of the inhabitants and destruction of the town of Boves, in what was described as an operation 'against anti-fascist partisans'. Hitler had ordered the division to Italy in July 1943, after Mussolini had been placed under arrest after being dismissed from office. The commander of Army Group Centre, Field Marshal von Kluge, was understandably irate at the thought of losing such an élite division from his order of battle, and he flew to Hitler's headquarters to protest. The Führer, however, merely stated the reasons why he was despatching his bodyguard: 'The point is I can't just take units from anywhere. I have to take politically reliable units. It is a very difficult decision, but I have no choice. Down there, I can only accomplish something with élite formations that are politically close to Fascism. If it weren't for that I could take a couple of army panzer division. But as it is, I need a magnet to gather the people together. To accomplish this I must have units down there which come under a political banner.' The presence of the *Leibstandarte* in Italy did act as a sort of magnet for committed fascists, but it had the opposite effect as far as the general populace was concerned. That said, it must be stated that the German Army also alienated the Italian population during its stay in Italy. Following the fall of Rome in June 1944, at a meeting of neo-fascist generals at Bergamo, it was reported that there was a 'great depression of a spiritual character after the fall of Rome'. There was also a big increase in the number of partisans in northern Italy. An order from Albert Kesselring, Commander-in-Chief, referred to the deterioration in the partisan situation and called for the utmost severity in dealing with them: 'Wherever there is evidence of considerable numbers of partisan groups, a proportion of the male population of the area will be arrested, and in the event of an act of violence being committed these men will be shot.' Of course the Waffen-SS would be less restrained than its army counterparts when carrying out these orders, but it does illustrate that the army could also carry out atrocities when ordered to do so. The *Leibstandarte* also took part in the disarming of the Italian Army following the overthrow of Mussolini's regime in September 1943, an act that was carried out with some severity by the Germans. Ironically the division saw no action against the invading Allied armies, being a private army for Mussolini, much to the disgust of its men, and it was a relieved *Leibstandarte* (a sentiment no doubt echoed by the Italians) which made its way back to the Eastern Front to fight the Red Army.

THE WARRIOR ÉLITE

The soldiers of the Waffen-SS were an élite, but those who won the Knight's Cross and its various grades were a higher brotherhood – the manifestation of the Nazi superman.

RIGHT: SS-Hauptsturmführer Michael Wittmann, the most famous tank ace of World War II, perhaps of all time. He received his first Tiger tank on the Eastern Front in early 1943, and thus embarked upon a remarkable career. The secret of his success was patience, often waiting for victims to come within close range. A member of the *Leibstandarte* Division, he was awarded the Knight's Cross, then the Oakleaves. In Normandy he fought as a member of I SS Panzer Corps, where he won the Swords for his outstanding actions against the British. By the time of his death on 8 August 1944, he had achieved 138 tank kills and 132 other vehicles destroyed.

LEFT: Knight's Cross of the Iron Cross with Oakleaves and Swords. On 15 July 1941, this award was introduced to reward continued acts of valour by Knight's Cross recipients. The design is basically the same as that of the Oakleaves, but with a pair of crossed swords attached to the bottom of the cluster. There were only 159 awards of this cluster made.

ABOVE: SS-Sturmbannführer Otto Skorzeny. Technically skilled and gifted in foreign languages, he was ordered to form a special commando unit, which rescued Mussolini in a daring raid from his Italian captors at the Gran Sasso Hotel in September 1943. Following the bomb plot against Hitler on 20 July 1944, he helped stop a possible mutiny among panzer troops in Berlin, but his most famous exploit was during the Ardennes Offensive, when his English-speaking soldiers caused havoc behind Allied lines.

ABOVE: SS-Brigadeführer Theodor Wisch, who joined the *Leibstandarte* in the spring of 1933. He was awarded the Knight's Cross in Russia as commander of the *Leibstandarte*'s 2nd Battalion, and won the Oakleaves as divisional commander. He led the division with such effectiveness during the battles in Normandy in June 1944 that he was awarded the Swords, becoming the 94th recipient. However, there is always a price to pay for such daring, and Wisch had to relinquish command in the autumn due to severe injuries.

ABOVE: SS-Brigadeführer Sylvester Stadler. Like many Knight's Cross winners, Stadler earned his award in the bitter battles on the Russian Front. He was then transferred to the Western Front to take part in the Ardennes Offensive. By this time he was the commander of the 9th SS Panzer Division *Hohenstaufen*, one of the crack units of the Third Reich, and the holder of the Oakleaves. He led the division until the war's end in May 1945, earning himself the Swords two days before the German surrender.

LEFT: SS-Obersturmbannführer Fritz Klingenberg, the man who captured Belgrade single-handedly in 1941. For this act of heroism (some would say foolishness) he was awarded the Knight's Cross by Hitler himself. He was killed in March 1945 while leading the 17th SS Panzergrenadier Division *Götz von Berlichingen.*

RIGHT: SS-Obersturmbannführer Max Wünsche, a member of the *Leibstandarte* Division who won the Knight's Cross for outstanding bravery during the battles around Kharkov in early 1943. He later won the Oakleaves as a panzer commander in the *Hitlerjugend* Division at Falaise.

CHAPTER THIRTEEN

Red Deluge

The campaign in Russia, 1943-44

Following the failure at Kursk German forces were on the defensive in the southern sector of the Eastern Front. Then they were pushed westwards as Red Army units smashed through the Mius defences and advanced towards Stalino and Taganrog. Field Marshal von Kleist and his Army Group A, on Manstein's southern flank, were in danger of being cut off.

LEFT: Russian infantry, armour and artillery race for the Dnieper in the second half of 1943. Note the officer on the left, seemingly oblivious to danger.

OPPOSITE: A Russian town burns as the Germans pull back in the face of the Red Army in August 1943, which hit the Wehrmacht like a thunder clap.

Manstein therefore shifted his reserves to assist Kleist, weakening his own forces so much that he was unable to resist the momentum of Vatutin's attack on the Voronezh Front. Kluge's Army Group Centre was also gradually pushed back towards Smolensk, its own problems too serious to allow it to assist Manstein. To the north, Model's 2nd Panzer Army was threatened with encirclement and was forced to withdraw across the neck of the Orel salient.

THE CRUMBLING FRONTLINE

By mid-August 1943, a massive gap had opened up in the German lines west of Kursk, and Soviet forces began to pour through it, threatening to take Kharkov once again. The *Wiking*, *Das Reich* and *Totenkopf* Divisions were all thrown into battle to prevent the loss of the city. But it was now the Red Army's turn to launch a massive pincer attack, with the 53rd Army driving in from the north and the 57th Army from the south – the 5th Guards Tank Army was to apply the *coup de grâce*. The Soviets ran into strong defences, and on just one day of fighting Waffen-SS anti-tank gunners knocked out over 180 Russian tanks. However, they could only delay the Red Army, and Manstein, fearing encirclement, ordered the city abandoned on 22 August.

Over the next few weeks *Wiking*, *Das Reich* and *Totenkopf* scored some outstanding successes in localised combats with armoured units of the Red Army. On 12 September, for example, *Das Reich* destroyed 78 enemy tanks in one engagement. However, the Russians could replace such great losses, whereas the Waffen-SS units found it increasingly difficult to maintain their own strength.

Hitler agreed to Manstein's Army Group South withdrawing to the line of Melitopol and the River Dnieper, thus retaining the western Ukraine in German hands. The withdrawal, undertaken in the face of Soviet pressure, was completed by 30 September. By that time a total of 68 German divisions – 1,250,000 men and over 2000 tanks of Army Group South – was tasked with holding the river line at all costs. Opposing them, however, the Red Army fielded a force almost twice as strong and in better shape.

THE FIGHTING WITHDRAWAL

In late August Soviet forces began to advance, and the Waffen-SS took part in a fighting withdrawal towards the Dnieper. Yelnya fell to the Red Army after two days of fighting, but the Russians had to battle all the way and had to pause within a week to regroup. Then the Red onslaught continued, capturing Bryansk, Smolensk and Roslavl, and by 2 October the Germans had been driven back almost 240km (150 miles).

In November 1943, the *Leibstandarte* was released from service in Italy and was sent back to the Eastern Front. It was allocated to XLVIII Panzer Corps of the 4th Panzer Army, situated to the south of Kiev, in the Ukraine. Despite the best efforts of the *Das Reich* Division, which was operating near Kiev, the city fell to the enemy on 7 November.

Between mid-November and the end of the year, both the *Leibstandarte* and *Das Reich* took part in a number of counterattacks as part of XLVIII Panzer Corps, but were unable to stop the Russian advance. The remaining division of II SS Panzer Corps, the *Totenkopf* Division, was rushed from one threatened sector of the front to another.

At the beginning of 1944 the Soviets attempted to smash German forces around Kirovgrad. They captured the town on 8 January 1944, but found German resistance stronger than expected. Some 11 German divisions were involved, including *Wiking* and the SS-Sturmbrigade *Wallonie*. The Russians realised that this German-held salient would have to be eliminated to ensure the success of the Soviet offensive. Koniev renewed his attack on 25 January, and by the 29th 60,000 Germans had been encircled near Cherkassy. The Soviets

BELOW: Soldiers of Army Group South fighting near Poltava in August 1943. Though the paper strength of Army Group South was 42 divisions, the reality was that most infantry divisions were at 20 per cent of their strength, while the army group as a whole had only 83 tanks and 98 self-propelled guns.

threw a ring of 35 divisions around the salient, and those inside appeared doomed. The only armoured unit in the pocket, the 5th SS Panzer Division *Wiking*, commanded by SS-Obergruppenführer Herbert Otto Gille, led the breakout. In a typical example of self-sacrifice, *Wiking*'s few remaining panzers turned back and held off the enemy for long enough to allow the last men to reach the German lines. Some 32,000 Germans escaped with their lives, and Manstein's Army Group South had been saved.

The *Das Reich* Division, now totally exhausted, was withdrawn from the front and sent to France for rest and refitting in February 1944. During March, Army Group South was forced to make a gradual withdrawal to the Dniester river, on the border with Romania. Elements of the *Totenkopf*, attached to XLVIII Panzer Corps, battled its way west to avoid encirclement. The exhausted SS men fought off the Soviet spearheads for three weeks, as the withdrawal continued through Balta and Romania. The Soviet offensive eventually ran out of steam, and the month of May was relatively peaceful. On 9 June, the division was pulled out of the line for some much needed rest and refitting, receiving sorely needed tanks and armoured vehicles, as well as 6000 men.

In March 1944, as Army Group South struggled to reorganise its left flank, it was struck by a new Soviet offensive which shattered it completely, tearing a massive gap between

the 1st and 4th Panzer Armies at Proskurov. Before the breach could be sealed, the entire 1st Panzer Army found itself surrounded in a pocket at Kamenets-Podolsk. At this point Hitler agreed to allow the reconstituted II SS Panzer Corps, which consisted of the élite 9th SS Panzer Division *Hohenstaufen* and the 10th SS Panzer Division *Frundsberg*, to be rushed to the Eastern Front. The escape from the pocket was achieved without serious losses; indeed, it is estimated that several hundred Soviet armoured vehicles were destroyed during the German withdrawal.

In April, the *Leibstandarte* was withdrawn from the East and moved to France for rest and refitting. *Hohenstaufen* and *Frundsberg* were held in reserve in Poland, and the *Wiking* Division, badly battered in the escape from the Cherkassy Pocket, was withdrawn from the front for rest.

THE BATTLE OF NARVA

In northern Russia in 1944, the Russians had lifted the siege of Leningrad, had gone on to the offensive and gradually drove the German armies westwards towards Estonia and Latvia. By the end of January, the Red Army had reached the German defence lines at Narva. So prominent were the foreign volunteer units of the Waffen-SS in this sector that the defence of Narva was to become known as the 'Battle of the European SS'.

Weeks of bloody fighting erupted in and around Narva, but the Waffen-SS refused to yield. By June 1944, for example, the Red Army had still not taken Narva, though the German bridgehead on the east bank, opposite the city, had been greatly reduced. The Germans, aware of the disasters befalling their comrades in the central and southern sectors of the front in Russia, realised that their position at Narva was becoming more precarious with each day, and so it was decided to pull back to a new defensive position further west, to the so-called Tannenberg Line.

On 24 July 1944, the northern prong of a massive pincer attack forced the 20th Waffen-Grenadier Division der SS back over the River Narva. The Estonian volunteers were forced to retreat westwards, fighting every inch of the way in defence of their homeland. Having experienced Soviet occupation once before, they had no wish to repeat it, and they fought tenaciously. On 24 July, the Waffen-SS units still on the east bank of the Narva slipped quickly over the river and into the city, destroying the bridges as they did so. By the close of the next day, the city itself had been evacuated. During the retreat to the Tannenberg positions, though, the Dutch unit General Seyffardt was cut off and annihilated by the Soviets.

On 26 July, the Russian assault at Tannenberg began. Subtle tactics were eschewed in favour of a massed assault on the greatly outnumbered Germans and the European volunteers. The fighting seesawed back and forth, first one side having the advantage then the other. Despite its many suc-

ABOVE: Hitler usually forbade withdrawal, but when he did sanction a retreat, orders went out to destroy everything of use to the enemy – food, bridges, railway lines and shelter – the policy of scorched earth. Here, SS pioneers detonate a charge on a railway line in southern Russia.

cesses, the Waffen-SS suffered great losses, while the enemy poured ever increasing numbers of fresh troops over the Narva and into the battle. The SS, for all its tenacity, was being bled white: virtually all its armour was gone, and its artillery was the only remaining heavy weaponry. The Russian attacks slackened somewhat in August, as the Red Army gathered its strength for one final all-out assault on the beleaguered Waffen-SS. The battered European volunteers could only await the mortal blow with apprehension.

By this time the European volunteers knew that the Soviet offensive was tearing holes in the front. For example, on 22 June 1944, the Red Army had launched its summer offensive across the entire front, codenamed 'Bagration'. The Red Army had built up a massive force of some six million men, compared to the Wehrmacht's two million. Army Group Centre, which would take the main brunt of the offensive, could field three-quarters of a million men, 1000 tanks and 10,000 artillery pieces. Opposing it, however, were over two million Red Army soldiers, 4000 tanks and 29,000 guns.

ABOVE: Some of the 2,633,000 Red Army troops committed by Stalin to shatter Army Group South after the Kursk Offensive. Manstein desperately tried to stem the Russian advance, and ordered the *Das Reich* and *Totenkopf* Divisions into the area west of Kharkov. They had two tasks: first, halting the enemy drive towards the River Dnieper; second, stopping Soviet armour from wheeling south and enveloping Kharkov from the west. For seven days the Waffen-SS divisions repulsed all attacks, but General Kempf in Kharkov abandoned the city in the face of certain defeat – Hitler dismissed him.

LEFT: A grim-faced crew of a Panzer IV rumble forward to take part in a counterattack in southern Russia in late 1943. German tactics were still superior to their Russian counterparts, but numbers were beginning to tell. Waffen-SS panzer units, in particular, imbued with ideological conviction and excellent training, achieved some remarkable victories. In August 1943, for example, *Das Reich*'s 2nd Company, equipped with Panthers, stopped an attack by 80 T-34s in a three-hour battle, destroying 23 enemy tanks.

RIGHT: 'Ivans' on the attack against Army Group Centre. The German Army, and Waffen-SS, were forced into a rethink concerning their foe during the course of the war in Russia. SS-Gruppenführer Max Simon, for example, commander of the *Totenkopf* Division, summarises his opinions thus: ' We found that no water or swamp was too deep and no forest too thick for them to find a way through. Other examples of infiltration were the appearance, in the latter part of the war, of officers in German uniform bringing fictitious orders.'

BELOW: German Panzer IVs in Zhitomir in late 1943. The dire strategic situation in southern Russia had necessitated Manstein throwing the Waffen-SS into the attack. The *Leibstandarte* and *Das Reich* Divisions, forming part of XLVIII Corps, launched a counterattack in the area between Kiev (which had fallen on 6 November) and Zhitomir. The corps retook Zhitomir on 19 November, with the *Leibstandarte* then turning east towards Brusilov. During this offensive tank ace Michael Wittmann destroyed six Russian tanks and five anti-tanks in the course of a morning's work.

LEFT: A concerned Himmler flanked by SS-Gruppenführer Otto Wächter, Governor of Galicia (left), and SS-Brigadeführer Fritz Freitag, commander of the 14th Waffen-Grenadier Division der SS (right). He has cause for concern. Despite Hitler's assertion that 'the Dnieper will flow backwards before the Russians overcome this powerful 800-yard-wide river line', by the end of 1943 the Red Army had breached the Dnieper line. Moreover, it now threatened the western Ukraine (Galicia).

BELOW: A German Schwimmvagen in muddy terrain, autumn 1943. The attrition suffered by Waffen-SS units during the almost continual fighting at this time is attested to by a member of the *Das Reich* Division in late September: 'Our machine guns kept up a continuous rain of fire and we changed our positions frequently to deceive the enemy as to how few we were.'

ABOVE: An abandoned German supply column on the Eastern Front, late 1943. All along the front the Germans were in retreat: in northern Russia, for example, Army Group North had sustained a shattering defeat, being forced back up to 272km (170 miles) in some places. The loss in military hardware had been enormous: 189 tanks, 1800 artillery pieces, 4660 machine guns and 22,000 submachine guns. In addition, partisan attacks had accounted for 300 bridges sabotaged, 136 military trains derailed and 1620 trucks destroyed.

BELOW: StuG III assault guns (left) and Hummel Self-propelled artillery in southern Russia in late 1943. The recall of the *Leibstandarte* from Italy, and its offensive with two fresh army panzer divisions, had briefly re-established the front in the south by mid-November, but the efforts of the Waffen-SS could only hold the Red Army momentarily. In December 1943 the Russians launched their great winter offensive, overwhelming Army Group Centre and steamrollering German units in their way – the writing was on the wall for the Third Reich.

TOTAL WAR

The war on the Eastern Front was conducted with ruthlessness and a disregard for the recognised rules of war. It was an ideological battle, in which the SS was in the van.

BELOW: Another Russian town burns. The losses suffered by the Wehrmacht in Russia were colossal, but then so were those suffered by the Waffen-SS. By 1943, one third of the original Waffen-SS divisions had fallen in Russia. Between 22 June and 19 November the formation had lost 1239 officers and 35,377 men, of whom 13,037 were killed. What was perhaps worse was that the quality of replacement sent by the training establishments was worryingly low.

RIGHT: The towns and villages are now only rubble, the result of over three years of war in Russia. Here, a German soldier scans the area for signs of the enemy. The Russians were very adept at urban fighting, and would always try to capture a single German soldier, after which they would torture him to force him to call out to his comrades to rescue him. But if they made an attempt to reach him they would be subjected to sniper and small-arms fire.

LEFT: Kreshchatik, Kiev's main street, following its liberation from the Germans in November 1943. The street has now been cleared of debris, allowing the free flow of traffic, including these pitiful refugees. The savagery of the war in Russia was in part the responsibility of Stalin, who in July 1941 demanded a policy of scorched earth to deprive the Nazi invader of shelter and food – 'What cannot be moved must be destroyed' – and as usual it was the Russian peasant who paid the price for this policy.

BELOW: 'The war against Russia will be such that it cannot be conducted in a chivalrous fashion. This struggle is one of ideologies and racial differences and will have to be conducted with unprecedented merciless and unrelenting harshness.' (Adolf Hitler to his senior officers, March 1941) This is the remains of the famous Pecherskaya Lavrai monastery in Kiev.

BELOW: Urabn fighting on the Eastern Front. Hans Woltersdorf, *Das Reich* Division, describes typical street fighting during the German attempts to hold Zhitomir in late 1943: 'There was a pause in the fighting and we took the opportunity to look into the first tank we had knocked out. The interior was sickening. A headless torso, bleeding flesh and guts splattered the walls. The men from the train told us that the driver was still breathing when they got him out of the machine ... now he lay dead, the back of his head had been smashed.'

RIGHT: Hitler visits the wounded in hospital in the company of his generals. These photo calls did much to raise the spirits of the Nazi faithful, but such scenes did nothing to endear the Waffen-SS to many young Germans, who were suffering heavy casualties at the front in Russia. Himmler lamented: 'In my view the overall conclusion is that the youth of our people has been clearly and deliberately poisoned by Christian education, particularly in wartime.'

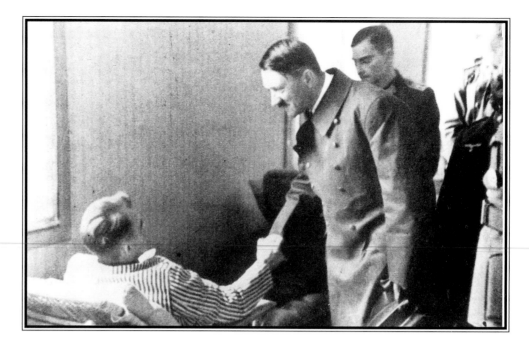

BELOW: A Soviet officer ambles among weapons and equipment abandoned by the retreating Germans. By the end of the third year of the war in Russia, the attitude of the individual Waffen-SS soldier was changing, as the historian Heinz Höhne states: 'With their faith in Hitler wavering, despairing of final victory, handicapped by second-rate reinforcements and wrestling with a crisis over the European volunteers, the SS army fell prey to ideological doubts, unsure whether it still belonged to the SS. The SS formations were now following their own banners and they were led by commanders whose loyalty to the leadership of the state was faltering.' This was probably true, but their oath of loyalty meant they would fight to the end.

ABOVE: A German 8.8cm anti-aircraft gun firing at Soviet tanks in February 1944. At the beginning of the campaign in Russia the German 3.7cm anti-tank gun proved to be totally inadequate against Russian tanks. Waffen-SS gunners were horrified to find their shells bouncing off enemy tanks. Some gun crews, frantically reloading and firing at point-blank range, were crushed beneath tank tracks or simply blown into pieces. The 8.8cm gun, however, was a formidable tank stopper.

LEFT: StuG III assault guns carrying grenadiers returning from a raid on the Eastern Front, January 1944. The Germans could always achieve localised successes, but by the beginning of 1944 the German Army had relinquished thousand of square kilometres of Russian territory. Against the weakened Army Group South the Red Army had massed 2,000,000 men, 51,000 artillery pieces, 2400 tanks and assault guns and 2850 aircraft. Manstein could call upon only half that in manpower.

THE CHERKASSY POCKET

In February 1944, for the first time since Stalingrad, large German formations were encircled, trapped in the Cherkassy Pocket. They were saved by the Waffen-SS.

BELOW: A German Panzer Iv is destroyed by Russian soldiers of the First Ukrainian Front in early 1944. By the beginning of February 1944, elements of the 1st Panzer and 8th Armies, which include the *Wiking* Division and Sturmbrigade *Wallonie*, were encircled around Korsun and Cherkassy – 75,000 men in all, plus all their equipment. Hitler, knowing that the Waffen-SS had held out in the Demyansk Pocket in 1942, forbade any attempts to break out westwards – General Stemmermann, the commander, would hold until Field Marshal Manstein could organise a relief force. However, it soon became clear that Manstein's units were in no condition to assemble such a force, and so Hitler, surprisingly, gave permission for the trapped units to break out of the pocket. The *Wiking* Division, being the only armoured unit in the pocket, was given the task of leading the thrust through the Russian lines, while the Sturmbrigade *Wallonie*, under the command of Lucien Lippert,

formed the rearguard. The Russians had positioned two entire tank armies between the pocket and German relief units to the west, in addition to other Red Army armoured units around the pocket. The break-out attempt began in mid-February, though it nearly ended in immediate failure as Russian tanks broke into the area between the 57th and 88th Infantry Divisions. To breach the gap the few remaining tanks of the *Wiking* Division turned back and hurled themselves at the Russian force. By doing so they had gained precious time to allow thousands of German troops to make their way westwards, but not one Waffen-SS tank survived the engagement – yet another instance of the reckless bravery of Waffen-SS soldiers in battle. During the rearguard battles Lippert had been killed, being replaced as commander of Wallonie by SS-Hauptsturmführer Léon Degrelle. By this time all vehicles had been destroyed, and all field pieces had been spiked.

ABOVE: At Cherkassy the Germans abandoned their vehicles when the roads became congested and the mud engulfed everything. When the snows came and the ground hardened carts were used, but then the horses were killed by enemy gunfire and shelling and the troops had to make their way on foot. The snowstorms that whipped the area on 16 February hid the thousands of troops, plus female signals auxiliaries, who trudged towards the west.

RIGHT: A dramatic photograph of a burning village in the Cherkassy Pocket. Against all the odds the Germans managed to break out west, but cruelly the stream at Gniloi-Tilkitsch had been turned into a raging torrent by the heavy rain and snow. As they forced their way across, the Russian pounded the German troops. The fighting was savage, and in the end only 34,000 troops reached the safety of German lines. The *Wiking* Division was down to 4000 men, while Sturmbrigade *Wallonie* had lost nearly 1400 men.

BELOW: Special badge for Single-Handed Destruction of a Tank, Silver Class and Gold Class. This badge was introduced on 9 March 1942. It was not for anti-tank troops but for other soldiers who destroyed an enemy armoured fighting vehicle single-handed, by means of a rocket, charge or grenade.

RIGHT: SS-Obersturmbannführer Vincenz Kaiser of the *Der Führer* Regiment, *Das Reich* Division. A tank killer *par excellence* (note the tank destruction badges on his arm), he fought on the Eastern Front, being killed in action on 20 April 1945 near Nuremberg.

BELOW: A knocked-out German Panther tank on the Russian Front. The Wehrmacht could ill afford such losses by early 1944. By March 1944, for example, the average Russian tank corps had around 50-100 tanks, whereas its equivalent, the panzer division, possessed no more than 30 fit for action. Both in men and hardware the Soviets were numerically superior.

ABOVE: A column of Waffen-SS troops gazes at a Russian T-34 tank in German service (note the large 'Balkan' cross painted on the side for recognition purposes). The war in Russia was bleeding the Waffen-SS white, but all Himmler could offer were empty platitudes: 'It is important that we all see before us an infinitely important task, never to allow the frontline of the Waffen-SS and the police to die out in any way. And if at some time we have to put the 16-year-olds, the 50-year-olds to arms, then we will do it. It is completely immaterial whether a year-entry bleeds more or bleeds less if it is a question of a whole Volk living. You can believe me, in every individual case, the many, many individuals of our worthy youth, the leaders and the men, who one knew and whom one has brought up oneself, cause one bitter sorrow and pain. But war is no matter of sentimentality. The war will be won because we have here the conflict between Europe and Asia ... and we will win.'

RIGHT: German Tank Battle Badges (note the numerals representing the number of engagements undertaken by the recipient). At first not numbered, it was given for taking part in three armoured assaults on three consecutive days, for having been wounded, or for winning a decoration in an assault. As the war progressed there was a need to recognise more engagement, leading to awards for 25 and 50, and 75 and 100 engagements.

CHAPTER FOURTEEN

Steel Rain

The Waffen-SS in the West, 1944-45

O n the eve of the Allied invasion of northwest Europe, four of the 10 German panzer divisions in France and Belgium were Waffen-SS. The *Das Reich* Division was initially stationed in the south of France near Toulouse, but was ordered north to the invasion front soon after D-Day, reaching the Normandy area by 10 July near Périers.

Allied forces initially maintained pressure at the eastern end of their bridge-head, one of the main objectives of General Montgomery's British 21st Army Group being the city of Caen. The first attempt to take the city was by direct assault on 6 and 7 June. The 12th SS Panzer Division *Hitlerjugend* moved into positions around Caen on 7 June and immediately formed an assault force to intercept the British forces. Under the command of SS-Standartenführer Kurt 'Panzer' Meyer, a battle group of three battalions of infantry and Panzer IV tanks from the division's panzer regiment, in conjunction with the Army's 21st Panzer Division, stopped the Allied assault. The advance was only temporary – the Germans were not strong enough to force the British infantry and armour to retreat.

MONTGOMERY IS FRUSTRATED BEFORE CAEN

By 9 June, Major-General Fritz Bayerlein and his Panzer Lehr Division were also in position around Caen, which meant that Caen and the vital Carpiquet airfield were now defended by three powerful panzer divisions.

Montgomery now decided to make use of two of his most experienced units: the 51st (Highland) Division and the 7th Armoured Division. The Scots were tasked with bypassing the 6th Airborne Division's positions east of the Orne river, while the 7th Armoured Division advanced against

LEFT: A destroyed American fuel dump during Hitler's Ardennes Offensive. German forces were suffering severe shortages of fuel by late 1944, and were issued with piping to enable them to siphon off any fuel from captured or disabled vehicles.

OPPOSITE: A German 3cm Flak anti-aircraft gun lends its support to an infantry attack during the fighting in Normandy, June 1944.

Caen from the northeast. In fighting lasting three days, however, the British made little or no progress, and the attack eventually petered out.

WITTMANN AT VILLERS-BOCAGE

On 10 June, the 7th Armoured Division attempted to force its way past the British 50th Division just to the west of Caen, but likewise made little progress. A gap in the German defences between Caumont and Villers-Bocage had been spotted by the British, and the 7th Armoured Division immediately attempted to exploit this, British armour entering Villers-Bocage on the morning of 13 June. At the same time, though, SS-Obersturmführer Michael Wittmann, commander of 2 Kompanie, schwere (heavy) SS-Panzer Abteilung 101, was also entering the village with a force of four Tiger tanks and one Panzer IV. Wittmann himself encountered four British Cromwell tanks on entering the village, and in a brief firefight knocked out three while the fourth tried to outflank him. However, it too fell victim to his deadly 8.8cm gun. Wittmann then rejoined the other Tigers and proceeded to attack an entire British armoured column from the 22nd Armoured Brigade. Driving along the side of the column, Wittmann knocked out a further 23 British tanks at point-

ed an even heavier attack and had withdrawn the 11th Armoured Division back across the Odon, so Hill 112 was soon back in German hands once again.

In Caen, the soldiers of the *Hitlerjugend* Division held on desperately, but the British eventually reached the Orne river, which ran through the centre of Caen. Then the *Leibstandarte* reached the front and took over the *Hitlerjugend*'s positions at Caen, allowing the 12th SS Panzer Division to go into reserve north of Falaise. On 18 July, the British launched Operation 'Goodwood', though the Germans quickly recovered from the three-hour bombardment, and tank and anti-tank fire soon began to exact its toll on Allied armour. Although the *Leibstandarte* was forced to relinquish most of Caen, the Allies lost over 400 tanks and the main German defence line was still relatively intact.

THE FALAISE POCKET

Fighting in other sectors was just as savage, but gradually Allied numerical superiority began to tell. The *Leibstandarte* and 2nd Panzer Division arrived in Argentan on 13 August, while *Frundsberg* was battling to hold back the Americans around Domfront. It soon became clear that only an immediate retreat through the Falaise-Argentan gap would save German forces in Normandy.

The *Hitlerjugend* Division desperately battled to hold open the gap. *Das Reich* and *Hohenstaufen*, which had both passed through the gap earlier, turned about and launched counterattacks against the Allies in a desperate attempt to gain time for their comrades trapped in the pocket. By the afternoon of 21 August 1944, the battle for the Falaise Pocket was over.

After the defeat of the German forces in Normandy, Field Marshal Montgomery persuaded Eisenhower to approve a combined ground and airborne assault through Holland entitled 'Market Garden'. This plan called for the capture of the bridges at Eindhoven and Nijmegen by US airborne forces, while the British would capture the furthest bridge at Arnhem. The assault was launched on 17 September, and II SS Panzer Corps under SS-Obergruppenführer Willi Bittrich, was put on alert. It consisted of the battered remnants of the once mighty 9th and 10th SS Panzer Divisions, both of which

blank range, as well as a similar number of half-tracks and lighter armoured vehicles. The shells of the British tanks merely bounced off the Tigers' massive armour plating, even at such close range.

By the time the four Tigers and Panzer IV returned through the village, however, British tanks and a 6-pounder anti-tank gun were waiting for them, and all five were knocked out by shots through their thinner side armour at close range. The panzer crews escaped. Nevertheless, Wittmann's action had saved the flanks of the Panzer *Lehr* Division, and for his achievements he was deservedly decorated with the Swords and Oakleaves to his Knights Cross.

OPERATIONS 'EPSOM' AND 'GOODWOOD'

By 14 June, the gap in the German lines had been sealed, and the 9th SS Panzer Division *Hohenstaufen* and the 10th SS Panzer Division *Frundsberg* were immediately ordered from Poland to Normandy. On reaching Normandy on 25 June, both divisions were fed into the line between Caen and Villers-Bocage. Their arrival was timely, coinciding as it did with Montgomery's Operation 'Epsom' (his attempt to take Caen). The British VIII Corps attacked along a 6km (four-mile) front between Carpiquet and Rauray. The Germans counterattacked on 27 June, but their assault was stopped in its tracks by the 11th Armoured Division, which then took the crucial Hill 112 on 29 June.

In reply, SS-Obergruppenführer Paul Hausser launched a major counterattack using both *Hohenstaufen* and *Frundsberg*, but the Waffen-SS soldiers were beaten back. Fortunately for the Germans, however, the Allies had expect-

had been decimated in the battle for Normandy. Nevertheless, they contained first-class troops, and their presence would come as a shock to the British 1st Airborne Division which landed at Arnhem .

At Arnhem the battle quickly degenerated into house-to-house and hand-to-hand fighting. On the morning of 19 September, an attempt by the bulk of 1 Para Brigade to force its way to the bridge was routed by German units. On 21 September, Major-General Stanislaw Sosabowski landed at Driel with the 1st Polish Parachute Brigade, to find himself faced with a German force which had by now decidedly gained the upper hand. The remnants of the British assault force were ordered to withdraw on the night of 25/26 September. The battered survivors withdrew over the Lower Rhine at Oosterbeek and retreated south.

THE ARDENNES OFFENSIVE

Towards the end of 1944 Hitler gathered his troops for what was to be his final attempt to regain the military initiative in the West: the ill-fated Ardennes Offensive, a three-pronged assault towards Antwerp. Its main strike component, the 6th Panzer Army under the command of SS-Oberstgruppenführer 'Sepp' Dietrich, was to attack through the Ardennes forests, force a crossing of the River Meuse between Liège and Huy, and then drive on towards Antwerp. General Hasso von Manteuffel, commander of the 5th Panzer Army, was to sweep northwest along Dietrich's southern flank, cross the Meuse between Namur and Dinant and push for Brussels, while the 7th Army, under General Erich Branden-berger, was to drive for the River Meuse.

The panzer element of Dietrich's 6th Panzer Army consisted of I SS Panzer Corps, whose principal components were the *Leib-standarte* Division and the 12th SS Panzer Division *Hitlerjugend*. In reserve was

RIGHT: An American column rumbles past destroyed German vehicles during the final stages of the fighting in Normandy in August 1944. The original caption for this photograph stated accurately: 'Our advance was terrific. They tried to stop us here and we blasted them right off the road.'

II SS Panzer Corps, comprising the 2nd SS Panzer Division *Das Reich* and the 9th SS Panzer Division *Hohenstaufen*. The infantry element comprised the 12th, 272nd, 277th and 326th Volksgrenadier Divisions and the 3rd Fallschirm Division.

The spearhead of the 6th Panzer Army was to be formed by I SS Panzer Corps, which was tasked with punching through the American lines between Hollerath and Krewinkel and driving through to the Liège-Huy sector, with the *Hitlerjugend* on the right flank and the *Leibstandarte* on the left. The lead in the attack of I SS Panzer Corps was given to a particularly powerful assault group. It was led by an officer who had proved himself in combat on numerous occasions: SS-Obersturmbannführer Joachim Peiper.

The offensive opened on the morning of 16 December 1944, but progress along the congested roads was slow. Kampfgruppe *Peiper* becoming entangled with slower-moving units. On 19 December, Peiper reached Stoumont, but the Allies were by now recovering from the initial shock of the attack and resistance was stiffening. *Hitlerjugend*, *Das Reich* and *Hohenstaufen* were all involved in an attack in the Manhay sector on 27 December, but failed to penetrate the American lines. By 24 January the situation in Hungary had deteriorated so seriously that all Waffen-SS divisions initially committed to the Ardennes Offensive were withdrawn and transferred to the crumbling Eastern Front. By 10 February 1945, the last German units were back over the River Rhine, and the Americans, Canadians, French and British continued their advance into the Reich itself.

LEFT: SS-Oberscharführer Ernst Barkmann, who joined the Waffen-SS on 1 April 1939, enlisting in the *Germania* Regiment. He fought in Poland and Russia, being wounded on the Eastern Front. In 1942 he volunteered for service with the panzer arm, being posted to *Das Reich*'s SS-Panzer Regiment 2. At the beginning of 1944 the division was transferred from Russia to Bordeaux for rest and refitting. When the Allies landed in Normandy, *Das Reich* was moved to the battle area and engaged the enemy. Barkmann and his crew created havoc with their Panther on American armour, knocking out around 50 enemy tanks. For his gallantry in Normandy he was awarded the Knight's Cross. He also fought in the Ardennes Offensive.

RIGHT: Camouflaged and heavily armed, four members of the 12th SS Panzer Division *Hitlerjugend* race towards the front in Normandy. Kurt 'Panzer' Meyer, who led the division in Normandy, stated of his young SS soldiers: 'The boys were educated to a sense of responsibility, a sense of community, a willingness to make sacrifices, decisiveness, self-control, camaraderie and perception ... Everything focused on training for battle.'

LEFT: Troops of the 1st SS Panzer Division *Leibstandarte* manhandle their equipment forward in Normandy. The SS was surprised by the ferocity and length of the artillery and aerial bombardments they had to endure at Allied hands, more ferocious than anything encountered on the Eastern Front. Such hammering took its toll: on 18 July, during a counterattack near Caghy, the *Leibstandarte* could muster only 46 armoured fighting vehicles and self-propelled guns.

RIGHT: Confident crew members of a *Hitlerjugend* Panzer IV in Normandy. The youths of the division fought with a fanaticism born of the National Socialist indoctrination they received as members of the Hitler Youth. As one 18-year-old member of the division wrote: 'We knew that we were quick, agile and confident. We trusted our officers and NCOs who had been hardened in battle. We had known them since the beginning of the training. During combat training with live ammunition we had enjoyed seeing them in the mud together with us.'

BELOW: A *Hitlerjugend* Panzer IV in action in Normandy. The division did not disappoint when it was committed to battle. Its first action was around Caen, where it fought a series of savage battles with Canadian forces. In these engagements casualties on both sides were heavy, with Meyer's regiment suffering 300 casualties in just a few hours' fighting.

ABOVE: SS-Hauptsturmführer Michael Wittmann, tank ace *par excellence*, and his crew during the Normandy battles. At this time Wittmann was commander of 2 Kompanie, schwere SS-Panzer Abteilung 101. His unit destroyed a British armoured column at Villers-Bocage on 13 June 1944, knocking out 27 tanks and a similar number of half-tracks and other armoured vehicles. Wittmann and his crew were killed on 8 August 1944 near Gaumesnil, just south of Caen. 'Panzer' Meyer wrote of him: 'Michael Wittmann died as he had lived – brave, dashing and a living example to his grenadiers.'

LEFT: Well camouflaged grenadiers of the *Hitlerjugend* Division in Normandy in June 1944 (note the sniper rifle). Field Marshal Rommel summed up the problem facing Waffen-SS and army units in the West after D-Day: 'It's not a matter of fanatical hordes to be driven forward in masses against our line ... here we are facing an enemy who applies all his native intelligence to the use of his many technical resources ... Dash and doggedness no longer make a soldier.'

LEFT: Two men of the *Leibstandarte* Division with their 8cm mortar during the Normandy battles in June 1944. By the 1930s the German Army had adopted mortars designed along the principles first devised by a British engineer, Sir Wilfred Stokes, in 1915. By World War II German mortar crews, including SS, were adept at setting up their weapons quickly, directing fire onto the enemy, and then getting out quickly before the opposition could organise counter-mortar fire.

BELOW: A German anti-tank gunner lies beside his knocked-out gun. In the background are three German tanks that have suffered a similar fate. The Waffen-SS suffered heavy casualties in Normandy, and by the conclusion of the campaign *Das Reich* had only 450 men and 25 tanks surviving, while the *Hitlerjugend* had 300 men, 10 tanks and no artillery.

ABOVE: Three Waffen-SS men sit on a British Army jeep following their capture during the campaign in northern France in 1944. The faces of the two young SS boys show disbelief at their predicament, while that of the older man in the centre registers an expression of grateful deliverance. Note his ribbon of the Iron Cross Second Class.

RIGHT: Fighting at Arnhem. A squadron of German tanks swings round in the street while covering a patrol of Waffen-SS men. Troops from both the 9th SS Panzer Division *Hohenstaufen* and 10th SS Panzer Division *Frundsberg* took part in the battles in and around Arnhem. Despite being under-strength due to their mauling in Normandy, they fought well. Contrary to popular opinion, the Waffen-SS soldiers were chivalrous towards their British captives after the battle.

LEFT: Men of the 6th Panzer Army advance during the Ardennes Offensive in December 1944. By this date attrition had taken its toll on the Waffen-SS. Dietrich, interviewed after the war, had the following to say about his panzer army: 'Replacements, for the most part, were from the air force, navy and other army units. Most of them were young men from 18 to 25 years of age. As unit training was carried up through battalion, but no higher, they were given only general training. The main trouble was lack of gasoline.'

BELOW: Troops of the 6th Panzer Army on the attack in the Ardennes. The German plan was to strike through the Ardennes forest, cross the Meuse and then strike for Antwerp. The *Leibstandarte* and *Hitlerjugend* Divisions were the spearhead units. In conjunction with the 6th Panzer Army, the 5th and 7th Panzer Armies would also attack, the overall aim being to break the Allies' front, cut off their supply line from Antwerp and save the Third Reich. As Hitler stated: 'Time is working against us, not for us.' What he did not know was that it had already run out for him and his empire.

RIGHT: A column of German prisoners is moved to the rear under the watchful gaze of American GIs. The Ardennes Offensive was beset with difficulties from the start. I SS Panzer Corps, for example, was faced by only a handful of inexperienced American troops, but they managed to cause a significant delay to the attackers. The American line was pushed back but it did not rupture, and so Dietrich was forced to commit the *Hitlerjugend* Division prematurely.

BELOW: The soldiers of the Waffen-SS fought with great determination in an effort to fulfil Hitler's wishes in the Ardennes, but to no avail. At the end of the first day of the offensive the Germans had lost the vital element of surprise. In addition, the weather, which had worked to the Germans' advantage during the assembly of forces and the denial of air cover to the Allies, now worked against them. The snow and rain made the going hard, as Dietrich explains: 'The 12th SS Panzer Division was attacking in swampy land, and it only had one part [100 litres] per tank. We thought this would be good for 50–60km [31.25–37.5 miles], but, in the swampy terrain, low gear had to be used quite a bit, and the gas didn't last. The division remained clogged up in this area [the Elsenborn Ridge] for three days and couldn't get started. Also, the American troops had many tank defences in the area, including tank traps.' Talking of the *Leibstandarte*: 'The division didn't have the gas it needed. It waited for fuel from 17 December to 19 December, but it didn't get any.'

LEFT: SS-Standartenführer Joachim Peiper, the commander of Kampfgruppe *Peiper* during the Ardennes Offensive. He served in the *Leibstandarte* in the West in 1940, and won the Knight's Cross at Kharkov in 1943. In the autumn of that year he took command of the *Leibstandarte's* panzer regiment and was awarded the Oakleaves. Leading his battle group during the ill-fated Ardennes Offensive, his men massacred 74 American prisoners at Malmédy, an offence for which Peiper and 42 of his men were sentenced to death after the war. However, his sentence was commuted to life imprisonment, though he was released in 1956. He changed his name and settled in France, but such individuals find it difficult to escape their past, and he was killed by former Resistance members on 13 July 1976.

RIGHT: Waffen-SS prisoners in January 1945. The Ardennes Offensive is over, and the Germans have lost. Nearly 100,000 of their soldiers have been killed, wounded or captured. The 5th and 6th Panzer Armies between them had lost 600 tanks, some divisions being left with fewer than 20 tanks. Most of the infantry divisions had been badly mauled, and ammunition was so low that there was enough for only five rounds each day for every gun in the West. These losses were made worse because they were irreplaceable – the Allies made good theirs in 14 days.

CHAPTER FIFTEEN

Circle of Fire

The end of the Third Reich

From August 1944 Romania and Bulgaria, Hitler's allies, left the Axis cause and sided with the Soviets. As Army Groups E and F, under Field Marshal von Weichs, were forced back through Yugoslavia, the ethnic volunteer SS divisions *Prinz Eugen*, *Skanderbeg* and *Kama* were decimated fighting Red Army units south of Vukovar in January 1945.

In Hungary, the capital Budapest came under the protection of General Otto Wöhler's Army Group South. Units committed to the defence of the city included the 8th SS Kavallerie Division *Florian Geyer*, 22nd SS Freiwilligen-Kavallerie Division *Maria Theresia* and 18th SS Freiwilligen-Panzergrenadier Division *Horst Wessel*.

THE DEFENCE OF BUDAPEST

In October 1944, the Hungarian head of state, Admiral Horthy, was about to join the Romanians and Bulgarians in leaving the Axis, but in a *coup d'etat* Horthy was overthrown and a puppet government loyal to the Nazis installed. At the beginning of the month, however, the Red Army had crossed the Hungarian border and raced for the Danube, reaching the river to the south of Budapest.

To the southwest of the city lay Lake Balaton, between which and the area around Budapest the Germans had established strong defensive positions. By 20 December 1944, the Soviets had advanced across the Danube and reached the southern shore of Lake Balaton. Marshal Tolbukhin diverted the main thrust of his attack past the eastern edges of Budapest, and with the 6th Guards Tank Army attacking from the northeast and the 46th Army from the south, the city was eventually encircled in a massive pincer action. Fighting

LEFT: Fighting in Berlin at the end of the war. The corpse of a Reichsarbeitsdienst (RAD) member lies on a street corner, while Red Army troops run past without a second glance.

OPPOSITE: The haggard face of a Waffen-SS grenadier in early 1945. He has seen many of his comrades killed in the efforts to keep back the Red Army – but to no avail.

raged for some time, the Soviets unable to rout the Germans and the latter unable to throw back the attackers.

On 26 December, IV SS Panzer Corps, comprising the 3rd SS Panzer Division *Totenkopf* and the 5th SS Panzer Division *Wiking*, were transferred from the Warsaw area in an attempt to relieve Budapest, but to no avail. The beleaguered garrison struggled on until 11 February 1945, when some 30,000 of the remaining troops inside the city attempted a breakout to the west. In the battles that ensued, the fleeing Germans were cut to pieces. *Florian Geyer* and *Maria Theresia* were annihilated, and Budapest surrendered on 12 February.

OPERATION 'SPRING AWAKENING'

The surrender of Budapest released a large number of Soviet troops for a new offensive on the German Army. As a consequence, the German-held oilfields at Nagykanizsa, Hungary, were in danger of being overrun by Soviet forces, which were now only 80km (50 miles) away. To stop this Hitler planned a new offensive, involving Army Groups South and Southeast. Army Group South, under General Wöhler, comprising the 6th SS Panzer Army, 8th Army, 6th Army and the Hungarian 3rd Army, would strike south from the Margarethe defence lines, while Army Group Southeast's 2nd Army would attack from the west of the Soviet lines. This pincer movement, it was hoped, would crush Tolbukhin's 3rd Ukrainian Front, comprising the 4th Guards Army, 26th Army, 57th Army and 1st Bulgarian Army. Meanwhile, IV SS Panzer Corps would remain in the Margarethe positions around Lake Balaton.

Commanded by SS-Oberstgruppenführer 'Sepp' Dietrich, the 6th SS Panzer Army consisted of the 1st SS Panzer Division *Leibstandarte*, 2nd SS Panzer Division *Das Reich*, 9th SS Panzer Division *Hohenstaufen* and the 12th SS Panzer Division *Hitlerjugend*. All newly arrived from the abortive Ardennes Offensive, they were substantially weakened. As a preliminary to the main attack, I SS Panzer Corps had smashed the Soviet bridgehead around Estergom with little difficulty. Once the Soviets became aware of a large body of élite Waffen-SS troops in the region, however, they quickly realised that a major offensive was indeed imminent and began to strengthen their defences accordingly, thickening up their minefields and preparing anti-tank defences.

THE RUSSIAN HAMMER BLOW

The offensive opened on 6 March. I SS Panzer Corps was best placed for the attack, the men having reached their positions in time, but II SS Panzer Corps was still floundering in the mud, its heavy vehicles finding the going almost impossible. The German attack began to suffer heavy losses almost from the start. Despite this, the Waffen-SS troops threw themselves into battle with their customary *élan* and determination, driving the Russians back, in the case of I SS Panzer Corps, for distances of up to 40km (25 miles).

The Soviet counteroffensive began on 16 March along the entire sector west of Budapest. Dietrich desperately reshuffled his forces to reinforce the areas most endangered, but

when he did so the Soviets soon swamped the areas from which the reinforcements had been taken. The 6th SS Panzer Army was in great danger of being completely cut off, as IV SS Panzer Corps struggled to maintain the German base line. *Das Reich* desperately battled to hold open a corridor of escape for its comrades, but the defection of the Hungarian Army left the flanks of II SS Panzer Corps wide open. By 25 March, the Russians had torn a 100km (60-mile) gap in the German defences.

As well as the four élite panzer divisions of the 6th SS Panzer Army and the two panzer divisions of IV SS Panzer Corps, the 16th SS Panzergrenadier Division *Reichsführer-SS* was also committed to battle around Lake Balaton. The *Horst Wessel* Division retreated into Slovakia. Within 10 days of the offensive being launched it had been totally wiped out.

HITLER TURNS ON THE WAFFEN-SS

Hitler was infuriated at this 'betrayal' by his élite Waffen-SS divisions when they failed to hold their positions, and demanded the removal of the cuff bands worn by these SS divisions as punishment for their offence. Dietrich, incensed by this insult to the gallantry and self-sacrifice shown by his soldiers, called a meeting of his divisional commanders, in which he informed them of Hitler's orders and then promptly ordered them to disobey.

The Soviet advance continued to the west of Budapest in a two-pronged movement towards Pápa and Győr. By 2 April, the Red Army had reached the Neusiedler Lake, on the border between Hungary and Austria, and two days later the last German soldiers had been driven out of Hungary. Of the Waffen-SS divisions which had fought in Hungary, most had withdrawn into Austria to defend Vienna. *Hohenstaufen* had been badly cut up in Hungary, and so its remnants were formed into small battle groups, which fought a rearguard action during the withdrawal towards Vienna. The *Totenkopf*, too, fought in defence

LEFT: Red Army officers view the advance of their troops over a makeshift river crossing in early 1945. Smoke and explosive shells fill the air around the soldiers, but nothing seems to be able to stop the inexorable Soviet advance into the Third Reich. At this time Guderian spoke of the Russian 'tidal wave'.

of the Austrian capital, while the *Hitlerjugend* withdrew into strong defensive positions around Wienerwald, to the south-west of the city, but was forced out of its positions by the unrelenting Soviet pressure after only a few days. *Das Reich* put up a stubborn defence to the south of Vienna, before being forced out of the city. *Reichsführer-SS* withdrew into Untersteiermark in the south of Austria.

By the spring of 1945, most of the so-called 'classic' Waffen-SS divisions were carrying out a fighting withdrawal through Hungary and into Austria, while in the central and northern sectors of the Eastern Front those SS units still in action were principally east and west European volunteer units. The level of determination shown by these volunteers in their attempts to hold the Soviet advance was quite exceptional, if not entirely surprising.

On 1 April, Stalin met his senior commanders to establish their plans for the final drive on Berlin. In the north was Rokossovsky with the 2nd Byelorussian Front, in the centre Zhukov with the 1st Byelorussian Front, and in the south Koniev with the 1st Ukrainian Front. The demarcation lines between the areas allocated to each front were to be relaxed some 65km (40 miles) from Berlin, and from then on it was to be a race to see which commander could reach the Reich's capital first.

Koniev ordered his 3rd and 4th Guards Tank Armies to break into the city on 20 April, but by the 23rd Stalin had declared that it was to be Zhukov's troops who would make the main assault. He then re-drew the boundaries within which the units were to operate in Berlin to give Zhukov's armies the honour of capturing the area, including the Führer bunker and the Reichstag.

THE FINAL BATTLE

By 25 April Berlin was completely surrounded, and the next day around half a million Red Army troops swarmed into the city itself. The battle for the city was a desperate one: savage hand-to-hand fighting in many places with knives, rifle butts and bayonets, and the Waffen-SS took part in the last, apocalyptic fight for the Third Reich. Ironically, most of those wearing SS uniforms were non-German volunteers. Apart from the host of Hitler Youth and Volkssturm personnel and two under-strength Army divisions of LVII Corps, the only other regular German troops in Berlin were the men of the *Nordland* and *Charlemagne* Divisions, a battalion of Latvians from the 15th Waffen-Grenadier Division der SS and 600 men of Himmler's Escort Battalion.

On 28 April, the Soviets broke through the inner city defences and stormed towards the Reichstag. As usual, the SS fought with great tenacity. The battered building had been turned into a fortress, with heavy machine guns and artillery emplaced behind makeshift gun ports. The first Soviet assault went in on 30 April, supported by artillery and Katyusha

ABOVE: German troops fall back through the rubble of what was once an affluent suburb of a German town in early 1945. By this time the Red Army possessed a superiority of 11 to one in infantry, seven to one in tanks and 20 to one in artillery pieces. And the Germans has wasted their reserves in the Ardennes.

rocket launchers. Three battalions of infantry charged forward in the face of heavy fire and managed to breach the defences. Inside the building the fighting degenerated into hand-to-hand combat. The SS had turned the cellar into a fortress, and it took two days of heavy fighting before they were defeated. Some 2500 of the Reichstag's defenders were killed, with another 2600 taken prisoner. By that time Hitler was dead and the battle for Berlin was over. At 1500 hours on 2 May, Lieutenant-General Weidling surrendered the city to the Russians. Although their Führer was dead and Germany's capital in Soviet hands, there were still groups of Waffen-SS troops fighting in various pockets of the shrinking Reich. They continued to fight until all the formal surrender negotiations had been completed.

As the Third Reich entered its death throes, Hitler had become increasingly contemptuous of those whom he considered had 'failed' him. Even the Waffen-SS had its limits, however, and when his élite troops also became unequal to the monumental tasks set for them, being usually overwhelmingly outnumbered, low on ammunition and food, and freezing without adequate winter clothing, their Führer had no sympathy for them. He heaped insult and scorn upon them, even his own bodyguard unit.

Even in defeat, though, the divisions of the Waffen-SS retained their distinctive characteristics. On 9 May 1945, *Das Reich*'s *Deutschland* Regiment sent the following message to headquarters: 'The Regiment *Deutschland* – now completely cut off, without supplies, with losses of 70 per cent in personnel and equipment, at the end of its strength – must capitulate. Tomorrow the regiment will march into captivity with all heads held high.' Thus ended the Waffen-SS's war.

ABOVE: The roads are once again turned into seas of mud as German StuG III assault guns retreat through a small rural hamlet in eastern Germany in early 1945. While the German Army and Waffen-SS had failed to stop the Russians, Himmler was convinced his 'Volk' could stop them: 'Each town block, each village, each farmstead, each trench, each copse, each wood will be defended by men, young lads and greybeards and – if it has to be done – by women and girls.'

LEFT: Waffen-SS panzergrenadiers take cover in a ditch while Ju 87 Stuka dive-bombers conduct an air strike against Red Army tanks. In the background can be seen German tanks, waiting to launch a counterattack once the air assault is over (note the turret hatches are open). On the Eastern Front, the brief lull at the end of 1944 was shattered in January 1945 as the Red Army broke out from its bridgeheads across the Vistula and surged westwards towards the frontier of the Third Reich itself.

LEFT: Two German soldiers await the next Russian attack in their bunker. Their weapons are Maschinenpistole 44 assault rifles, while on the ground lay two stick grenades. The MP 44 had a magazine capacity of 30 rounds and a cyclic rate of fire of around 800 rounds a minute. It was developed as a result of the early Russian campaigns and the need for a good assault weapon, but it came too late to make a difference to the outcome of the war. Many Waffen-SS soldiers were issued with MP 44s during the final battles of the Third Reich in 1945.

BELOW: German Nebelwerfer rocket launchers mounted on armoured cars on the southern sector of the Eastern Front in January 1945. The armoured version of the Maultier half-track seen here is carrying 10 15cm Nebelwerfer rocket tubes. Note the horse and cart, tow items that still played an important part in military operations in the East. The Soviet ring around Budapest at this time prompted Hitler to order a relief attack, made up of the *Totenkopf* and *Wiking* Divisions. The attack was scheduled for New Year's Day, but Guderian was sceptical: 'Hitler expected great results from this attack. I was sceptical since very little time had been allowed for its preparation and neither the troops nor the commanders possessed the same drive as in the old days.' Guderian was right, for although the two Waffen-SS divisions fought for 10 days against the Soviet 4th and 6th Guards Tank Armies, they suffered such losses that the attack was called off.

LEFT: The Red Army on the way to Germany. For the Waffen-SS the war in the East had been a crusade: National Socialism versus Bolshevism, the Herrenvolk (master race) against the Untermenschen (sub-humans). By 1945 the unthinkable had happened: the supermen had failed and were losing the war. The Soviet offensive of January 1945 was massive in its intensity and scope. It was a repeat of the German Blitzkrieg, but in reverse, and with such resources as the Wehrmacht had never enjoyed, and within 14 days it had reached Germany.

RIGHT: A Waffen-SS observer radios information to the panzer squadron commander. Two of the tanks, Panzer V Panthers, can be seen in the background. In January 1945 the Red Army's first priority had been to clear the Germans out of Poland, which it did, though having to fight hard. As the Germans pulled back into East Prussia they still had nearly 1,000,000 troops, but facing them were over 2,000,000 Russian troops, 14,000 tanks and over 60,000 artillery pieces.

LEFT: Two SS men walk through a forest in Belgium near the German border, soon to be occupied by the Allies. The front was crumbling in both the East and West, though in desperation SS-Obergruppenführer Hans Prützmann, who had been SS Police Chief in the Ukraine from 1942 until 1944, organised so-called 'Werewolf' units on Himmler's behalf. These were supposed to carry out sabotage operations against the Allies, but in the event the idea never got off the ground. However, it does illustrate how far the Nazi hierarchy had become detached from reality in the final days of the Reich. The only tangible result was in alarming Allied soldiers into a more hostile attitude towards the German people.

LEFT: A Waffen-SS patrol in what had been in former times an elegant German town square. By this time Himmler had a new oath for his SS to spur them on to even greater efforts: 'First, we must swear that, like our fathers, we want to be loyal, loyal to the Führer, whom the Lord God has sent us, loyal to the Reich which unites all Germans ... Loyal to the Volk and thereby to ourselves, because we are the most valuable elements to defend and preserve the eternal life of the Germanic peoples, its women and children, and therewith its blood.'

BELOW: A Waffen-SS soldier, MP 40 in his hand, peers round a corner of a house during street fighting in eastern Germany, April 1945. His comrade is armed with a Einstossflammenwerfer 46 flamethrower, which consisted of a hollow tube containing fuel and a gas cartridge for a single burst.

RIGHT: SS troops trudge through the burned-out street of yet another destroyed town in eastern Germany. The closer the Red Army got to Berlin the more unrealistic Hitler became, ranting: 'Whatever the enemy does, he can never reckon on a capitulation. Never! Never! Never!'

RIGHT: Even after the end of the Third Reich the Waffen-SS honoured those within its ranks who had performed acts of bravery. This is the confirmatory attestation from SS-Standartenführer Léon Degrelle, commander of the 28th SS Freiwilligen-Panzergrenadier Division *Wallonien* (though it never exceeded regimental strength), relating to Jacques Leroy's Knight's Cross. In January 1945 the division was put into the line at Stettin, where after heavy fighting it was reduced to 700 men. What was left of the division ended the war in Denmark.

LEON DEGRELLE

Madrid, le 8 Décembre 1973.

Attestation

Je soussigné Léon Degrelle, né à Bouillon le 15 Juin 1906, déclare certifié que le nommé :

LEROY, Jacques, né à Binche le 10 Septembre 1924, a obtenu la Ritterkreuz sur le Front de Stettin, à Altdam, le 20 Avril 1945.

S.S. Standartenführer
et Commandeur de la 28ème SS. Division "Wallonie"

BELOW: SS-Unterscharführer Thomas Hellor Cooper, a Briton who was a member of the Waffen-SS, the only Englishman to win a German combat decoration, on the Eastern Front. He ended the war as a member of the British Free Corps. Tried for treason at the Old Bailey, his death sentence was commuted.

BELOW: The battered face of the Waffen-SS in 1945 – SS-Untersturmführer Jacques Leroy. Awarded the Knight's Cross for his bravery (see above), it was not until 8 December 1973 that this Walloon was confirmed as being a Knight's Cross winner by the divisional commander, Léon Degrelle.

RIGHT: Attestation, dated 20 May 1957, from Roger Wastiau, affirming SS-Untersturmführer Jacques Leroy's entitlement to the Knight's Cross (Wastiau was the adjutant of the *Wallonien* Division). Typical of the calibre of the average Waffen-SS soldier, Leroy had won his award after losing his eye in combat. Terribly injured, he nevertheless left his hospital bed and rejoined his unit fighting on the Eastern Front. By April 1945, though, such superhuman efforts were in vain.

Bruxelles, le 20 mai 1957

A T T E S T A T I O N
===

Je soussigné WASTIAU , Roger , né à Grammont le 30
octobre 1921 , et domicilié à Bruxelles II, rue de
l'Industrie, déclare certifié que le nommé :
LEROY, Jacques ,né à Binche le 10 septembre 1924
a obtenu la Ritterkreuz sur le Front de Stettin, à Altdam
le 20 avril 1945 .

SS. Hauptsturmführer
ù. Div. Adjudant

LEFT: A different world. The halcyon days of Himmler's empire: an Allgemeine-SS man with four British League of Fascist members in 1935. Ten years later even the SS was demoralised. In January 1945, the SS's propaganda unit filed this report to Himmler: 'The mood in the fighting troops due to the events on the Eastern Front becomes more nervous and serious by the day ... Should the situation deteriorate further in the next few days it is to be expected that the troops will no longer be able to bear the anxiety and their fighting spirit will be paralysed ... The mood in the local population is, apart from the unthinking, similar.' Himmler's ludicrous reply was thus: 'The troops must be told that, bitter as it is, they must do their duty now more than ever, and only if the West is guarded now will the German forces in the East be in the position first to parry the thrust and then to become active again.'

ONE MAN'S WAR

SS-Untersturmführer Georg Müller, an early member of the SS who served throughout the war. He was but one of thousands who served in the Black Corps.

LEFT: Müller's SA Wehrsportabzeichen certificate book. Sports were very important in the SS. Himmler believed sport 'recognises the élite and eliminates the weak'.

ABOVE: Georg Müller in his black Allgemeine-SS uniform. His cap has the early form of the Nazi cap eagle. Müller served the Nazi Party for nearly 20 years, losing his leg in action in Russia.

RIGHT: The obverse of Müller's NSDAP membership card. This card, issued on 15 November 1931, relates to his own particular cell of the organisation *Ortsgruppe Duisburg*. It is extremely rare for such a significant group of documents and photographs illustrated on these two pages to survive intact. That they did survive was down to Müller hiding them in his artificial leg at the end of the war. Müller was definitely a product of the Nazi system, one of those 'tough youths' whom Himmler continually spoke of and admired.

IM NAMEN DES FÜHRERS
UND
OBERSTEN BEFEHLSHABERS
DER WEHRMACHT

IST DEM

Leutnant
Georg Müller

AM 5.9.1942

DIE MEDAILLE
WINTERSCHLACHT IM OSTEN
1941/42
(OSTMEDAILLE)

VERLIEHEN WORDEN.

FÜR DIE RICHTIGKEIT:
Gren.-Erf.- Btl. 107

Major u. Btl.-Kommandeur

Schutzstaffeln der N.S.D.A.P.

SS-Führer-
Ausweis Nr. 4 700

Pg. Müller, Georg

Mitglieds-Nr. 46 581

SS-Untersturmführer

in der Stammabt.West Bez.25

Eigenhändige Unterschrift

IM NAMEN DES FÜHRERS

VERLEIHE ICH
DEM

Oberleutnant
Georg Müller
I./F.A.Rgt.1308

DAS

KRIEGSVERDIENSTKREUZ
2. KLASSE
MIT SCHWERTERN

Div.Gef.Std., DEN 20.April 1945

(DIENSTSIEGEL)

Generalmajor u.Div.Kdr.
(DIENSTGRAD UND DIENSTSTELLUNG)

ABOVE: Award document for the Eastern Front Medal earned by Leutnant Georg Müller while he was fighting in Russia in the winter of 1941-42. Müller had associations with various branches of the Nazi Party, including membership of the Allgemeine-SS. He joined the German Army during the war and won a number of awards for his conduct in battle. These documents illustrate the highly regimented nature of Nazi Germany, its obsession with documents and official paperwork. Ironically, the comprehensive records and identification were to trap many SS members as they tried to flee Germany in disguise following Germany's defeat in May 1945.

ABOVE: The obverse of the SS officer's ID card, issued to Georg Müller in 1936. The card is printed on white card stock with a grey eagle and swastika watermark, which was an additional security measure to deter forgery. It contains basic information regarding the holder, such as party number and rank.

LEFT: Award document for the War Service Cross Second Class with Swords, given to Müller on Hitler's birthday (20 April 1945), less than three weeks before the end of the war. By this time Müller had been promoted to oberleutnant. Had it not been for his artificial leg he would have been 'relieved' of his documents by the Russians.

LEFT: A column of Red Army tanks rumbles through Berlin in May 1945. Ironically, the final Battle of Berlin was conducted by foreign members of the Waffen-SS, who were to die defending Hitler and his entourage. These men were members of the *Nordland* Division, *Charlemagne* Division and a battalion of Latvians from the 15th Waffen-SS Division.

BELOW: Thick black smoke hangs over the capital of the Third Reich as Soviet troops run across the debris-strewn square in the very heart of Berlin. Russian estimates of German losses during the last three months of the war in the East were 1,000,000 killed, 800,000 men, 12,000 tanks and 23,000 artillery pieces captured.

RIGHT: Russian soldiers pose in front of the Brandenburg Gate in Berlin following the German surrender. Hitler is dead, shot by his own hand, while much of Europe lays in ruins. The Waffen-SS is a defeated formation. Within the German High Command there was concern as to how it would react to orders to surrender. However, 'Sepp' Dietrich decided to obey orders – there was to be no last, glorious stand. For thousands of SS soldiers, the future held the prospect of long imprisonment.

BELOW: 'It is untrue that I, or anybody else in Germany, wanted war in 1939. It was wanted and provoked exclusively by those international politicians who either came of Jewish stock, or worked for Jewish interests. After all my offers of disarmament, posterity cannot place the responsibility for this war on me ... If the war is lost the German nation will perish. There is no need to take into consideration the basic requirements of the people. Those who will remain after the battle are those who are inferior; for the good will have fallen.' (Adolf Hitler, April 1945) The shot-pummelled Reichstag lies in ruins, while only a short distance away is Hitler's bunker. SS-Oberführer Wilhelm Mohnke set fire to the bunker the day after Hitler's suicide, and then joined one of the escape groups that night. He was later captured by the Russians while hiding in a cellar.

CHAPTER SIXTEEN

Consequences of an Ideology

Many former members of the Waffen-SS tried to maintain after the war that it had committed no more atrocities than any other military formation. But the Waffen-SS was too large and diverse an organisation for such a sweeping statement to apply. Even the early Waffen-SS divisions were not of an equally high standard. The 4th SS *Polizei* Division, for example, was equipped to a lower standard than its counterparts, as was the 7th SS Gebirgs Division *Prinz Eugen*, both being used primarily for anti-partisan duties and being allocated a degree of obsolete and captured equipment.

Those Waffen-SS divisions which were considered to be the true élite did indeed come from the first half of the SS order of battle. Divisions such as the *Leibstandarte*, *Das Reich*, *Wiking*, *Hohenstaufen*, *Frundsberg*, *Hitlerjugend* and *Götz von Berlichingen* all earned enviable reputations for military prowess, but what of the atrocities they committed?.

THE FIRST WAFFEN-SS CRIMES

Undoubtedly the most famous of the Waffen-SS divisions was the *Leibstandarte* Division, which grew to become one of Germany's most powerful armoured formations. Military training was carried out using the very latest tactics, and officers and men went through it together. By the time the war began the *Leibstandarte* Division was a first-class fighting formation – well equipped, well trained, supremely confident and with morale second to none.

Almost from the start of hostilities in September 1939, Waffen-SS soldiers gained a reputation for reckless gallantry when compared to their army colleagues. And from the start atrocities were commited. It was in Poland that the first recorded Waffen-SS atrocity occurred on 19 September 1939. An SS soldier called Ernst, of the SS-Artillery Regiment, and

LEFT: Concentration camp inmates leave Dachau to spend Christmas at their homes. Such philanthropy soon evaporated.

OPPOSITE: A Soviet soldier hanged by the Waffen-SS for 'crimes against the Third Reich', a scene repeated countless times in Russia.

an Army policeman herded 50 Jews into a synagogue and shot them. The SS soldier was then court-martialled, the prosecutor demanding the death penalty. However, a senior judge in Germany quashed the death sentence, saying that the SS soldier 'was in a state of irritation as a result of the many atrocities committed by the Poles against ethnic Germans. As an SS man he was also particularly sensitive to the sight of Jews and the hostile attitude of Jewry to Germans; and thus acted quite unpremeditatedly in a spirit of youthful enthusiasm'.

THE WESTERN CAMPAIGN

The *Leibstandarte* Division was expanded for the attack in the West in 1940, and took part in the drive through Holland and into France, pushing towards the Channel coast at Dunkirk. On 27 May 1940, a number of British soldiers who had been captured by the Waffen-SS were herded into a barn near the village of Wormhoudt and killed by grenade and small-arms fire. The perpetrators maintained that one of the prisoners had concealed a revolver, which he used to fire at them, thus provoking the shooting. No conclusive evidence to support this version of the events of that day have ever been produced, and the killings must remain a blot on the reputation of the *Leibstandarte*. In contrast, when the *Leibstandarte* subsequently met up with British forces again during the German invasion of Greece in 1941, some of those British troops captured went to great pains to record their chivalrous treatment by their Waffen-SS captors.

the prisoners were killed. This was clearly a crime for which the perpetrators would have to be brought to justice. The controversy arose over the way in which the investigations were handled. The Americans sought to show that this massacre was the result of a German policy decision not to take prisoners. The order was said to have emanated from SS-Oberstgruppenführer Josef 'Sepp' Dietrich.

War in the East introduced the young Waffen-SS grenadiers to a far more brutal and unrelentingly savage form of warfare. The SS had been taught to regard the Russians as despised and hated communist enemies, anathema to all that National Socialism stood for. The Soviets, on the other hand, saw the Germans as hated fascist invaders. This mutual aversion expressed itself on the field of battle in fierce hand-to-hand fighting, with no quarter being asked or given. What may be acceptable in the heat of battle, however, is an entirely different matter outside combat, and the *Leibstandarte* was accused of the cold-blooded murder of a large number of Soviet prisoners of war in October 1941 during the battle for Taganrog. The *Leibstandarte*'s commander, 'Sepp' Dietrich, did give an order that for a period of several days no enemy prisoners were to be taken, in reprisal for Soviet atrocities against his own men.

THE MALMÉDY MASSACRE

During the Ardennes Offensive in late 1944 the Waffen-SS again committed an atrocity. A number of American prisoners had been assembled at the Baugnez crossroads, near Malmédy, as spearhead units of I SS Panzer Corps streamed past. They were guarded by two tanks and their crews. German sources claim that only some 20 prisoners were involved, Belgian witnesses say around 35, and the Americans claim over 120. Whatever the numbers involved, a crewman in tank number 731, a Romanian Volksdeutsche named Georg Fleps, fired his automatic pistol into the mass of prisoners. As they scattered the other Germans opened fire and most of

After the war some 500 Waffen-SS soldiers from I SS Panzer Corps, including Dietrich, SS-Gruppenführer Hermann Priess, commander of the *Leibstandarte*, and SS-Obersturmbannführer Joachim Peiper, commander of the spearhead unit, Kampfgruppe *Peiper*, were imprisoned.

WHAT VERDICT FOR THE WAFFEN-SS?

As Germany's war machine slowly disintegrated, it was invariably the élite Waffen-SS units that were rushed in to fill the gaps in the Reich's crumbling defences. The almost continuous combat and fierce actions resulted in high casualty rates, yet the esprit de corps of most of the élite Waffen-SS units remained undiminished. By this time many of these Waffen-SS soldiers had become hardened cynics, with no real feelings of loyalty to their political masters or their Reichsführer-SS; their loyalty instead being directed towards their comrades and their unit. In this sense these Waffen-SS grenadiers had become very much like the Freikorps soldiers of the 1920s. Himmler's blundering attempts at military leadership – Hitler made him commander of Army Group Vistula – had shown him totally incompetent to lead an army in the field, and had earned him the contempt of many of his battle-hardened Waffen-SS troops.

Whatever the merits or otherwise of the Waffen-SS divisions as fighting formations, there is no doubt that a greater proportion of war crimes were alleged to have been committed by them than by any other branch of Germany's armed forces. Clearly, in the case of some of the so called 'classic' divisions at least, the bulk of any excesses which they have been charged with were carried out in the heat of battle by only a small element, and often in response to similar excesses being carried out by the enemy. Even Simon Wiesenthal, the investigator of Nazi war crimes, has stated his opinion that, during the early years of the war at least, a man serving in the Waffen-SS had neither more nor less to answer for than any other German soldier.

THE DECISION OF NUREMBERG

Clearly, for much of the SS there can be no redeeming factors. The International Military Tribunal at Nuremberg stated that the SS 'was utilised for purposes which were criminal under the Charter [of the International Military Tribunal], involving the persecution and extermination of the Jews, brutalities and killings in concentration camps, excesses in the administration of occupied territories, the administration of the slave-labour programme and the mistreatment and murder of prisoners of war.' It also went on to record that the Waffen-SS 'was in theory and practice as much an integral part of the SS organisation as any other branch of the SS', and it was 'directly involved in the killing of prisoners of war and the atrocities in occupied countries. It supplied personnel for the Einsatzgruppen, and had command over the concentration camp guards after its absorption of the Totenkopf SS.' As such, it thus had complicity in the extermination of six million Jews, hundreds of thousands of slave labourers and the murder of untold numbers of civilians in eastern Europe.

No one could possibly seek to condone or justify the actions of the Einsatz-gruppen (SS Special Action Groups), the Gestapo, the SS-Totenkopfverbände (concentration camp guards) and others. In addition, it is inconceivable that history will ever consider that it has

RIGHT: Concentration camp inmates in their blue and white-striped uniforms crowd round a stove in their block. Theodor Eicke, head of concentration camp guards, believed the camps were the 'most effective instrument available for destroying the enemies of National Socialism'.

been unjust in its treatment of some of the Waffen-SS units, such as the notorious Moslem volunteers or the Ukrainian auxiliaries who served in the police units or as concentration camp guards. Those units must go down as monstrous aberrations. Their claim to be soldiers like any others must be rejected absolutely.

Those soldiers from the élite units of the Reichsdeutsche Waffen-SS and some of the Germanic volunteers, however, can probably be justified in claiming the right to be considered soldiers like any others, even if this consideration is not accorded to the Waffen-SS as a whole. These troops were not involved in genocide or crimes against humanity on a divisional basis, but were nevertheless soldiers who were imbued with the tenets of National Socialism and all its hare-brained racial theories.

That said, for units such as the *Totenkopf* Division, with its ruthless ideological indoctrination and links with the concentration camps, the waters become murky. Thus the 'classic' Waffen-SS divisions are guilty when it comes to atrocities, or at the very least of collusion in murder. In April 1941, for example, one of the companies of the *Das Reich* Division assisted an SS extermination squad in shooting 920 Jews near Minsk. The same division was involved in the killings at Oradour-sur-Glane in France in 1944. There are just too many of such instances for the Waffen-SS to escape condemnation.

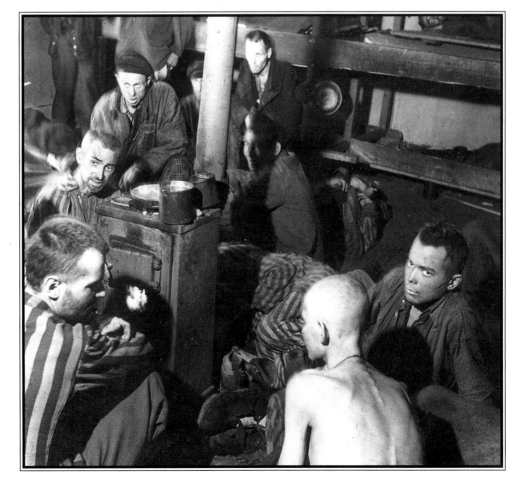

RIGHT: 'We have very, very many against us, as you yourselves as National Socialists know very well. All capital, the whole of Jewry, the whole of freemasonry, all the democrats and philistines of the world.' (Heinrich Himmler) Here, a Jew, one of the 'enemy' is searched for valuables or 'hidden arms' before being sent to a ghetto, from where he will eventually be sent to a concentration camp, if he hasn't been starved or worked to death first, or simply killed by a guard.

LEFT: The Zoll Fahndungsdienst disc, issued for the Customs Inspection Service of Bremen. The Customs Service was subject to the control of the Gestapo, and as such was involved in the rounding up of Jews and other enemies of National Socialism.

BELOW LEFT: Staatliche Preussisch Kriminal Polizei warrant disc. Such items seem innocuous enough now, but any suspect shown one would be stricken with terror at the thought of being taken to police headquarters for questioning, a journey that could be one way only.

BELOW: Three Jewish prisoners are investigated by a member of the Sicherheitsdienst (SD), the Nazi Party's intelligence and security body. The SD was headed by Heydrich, a fanatical anti-Semite who devised the 'final solution of the Jewish problem'.

RIGHT: Governor Dr Hans Frank, Governor-General of occupied Poland, surrounded by Waffen-SS officers during an inspection tour on the Eastern Front in 1942. It was on such tours that the final resting place of the Jews was determined. The presence of Waffen-SS officers on such tours shows the claims of Waffen-SS soldiers that they knew nothing of the policy of mass murder against Jews and others to be false. Indeed, when called upon to do so Waffen-SS units took part in murder – their blind obedience dictated so.

LEFT: Prisoners await their fate at the hands of an SS firing squad. The two in the foreground beg for mercy, to no avail. The hearts of the SS men are hardened to such pleas. At the beginning of the Russian Campaign in 1941, SS and Einsatzgruppen units followed the German armies, rounding up those who did not fit into the Nazi scheme of things for execution. The first method was mass shooting. One SS NCO, participating in the execution of Russian Jews, wrote in his diary of such actions: 'What can they be thinking? I believe each still has the hope of not being shot. I don't feel the slightest pity. That's how it is and has got to be.'

RIGHT: Neat lines of bodies, ready for transportation to a mass burial site or the crematoria of a concentration camp. It has never been satisfactorily explained how, during so-called Waffen-SS anti-partisan operations, innocent men, women and children were murdered, as at Minsk, Kharkov, Boves in Italy, Klissura in Greece and Oradour in France. Only by taking into account the Waffen-SS's contempt for life can it be explained, but never justified.

LEFT: A detail of Order Police on their way to exterminate a group of Polish Jews. The shovels will be given to the Jews, who will be forced to dig their own graves.

BELOW: Concentration camp inmates toiling in a quarry. Considered expendable, their SS guards knew how to extract the most from them before they died.

LEFT: An identity disc for the dreaded Gestapo, the secret police of the Third Reich. Dressed in civilian clothes, Gestapo agents were authorised to extract confessions by force. At its height it had 45,000 men and 100,000 informers.

LEFT: An incongruous picture of concentration camp prisoners manufacturing munitions for the Reich (uniforms for the Waffen-SS were also made in the camps). Inmates contributed to all war work, including the building of V-1 and V-2 rockets. Any infringement of the strict codes applied to their employment resulted in summary execution. Any sabotage was dealt with equally harshly, with the whole shift being exterminated. Such measures kept prisoners in line.

RIGHT: Jews murdered in Poland in 1939 by members of what was later to become the *Totenkopf* Division. Eicke's *Brandenburg* Regiment moved into Poland in September 1939 to begin so-called 'cleansing and security measures'. The commander of the regiment, SS-Standartenführer Paul Nostitz, reported to Eicke that he had arrested and shot large numbers of 'suspicious elements, plunderers, insurgents, Jews and Poles'. Thousands were killed.

LEFT: More innocent people shot by the SS, this time in Russia. Whole communities were taken out and shot by the Einsatzgruppen, sometimes purely on a whim. One account states that the SS officer in charge got in touch with headquarters for guidance in regard to a group of civilians he was holding, as he *thought* (author's italics) that they did not qualify as being classed as 'sub-human'. The reply he received was simple: if there was the slightest doubt as to their racial purity they were to be exterminated.

RIGHT: It was strictly forbidden for members of the German armed forces to take private photographs of public executions. Here, though, a mixed group of soldiers crowd round to witness the fate of a Russian partisan. Those taking photographs seem to be unconcerned as to orders. Such instances also contradict the often-touted view from former SS and army soldiers that they knew nothing of executions and atrocities during the war. Even if they did not partic-ipate in such actions, they undoubtedly knew what was going on.

HELL ON EARTH

The brutality and inhumanity practised in the Third Reich's concentration camps is hard to comprehend, much less that it went on for nearly 20 years.

ABOVE: The torture devised by SS-Oberführer Hans Loritz, commandant of Dachau. Prisoners had their hands tied behind their backs and then suspended from a post as shown. After, a victim would be unable to move his arms for weeks.

ABOVE: An SS-Standartenführer lectures SS-Totenkopfverbände men on their duties at the Dachau camp. Under the guidance of Theodor Eicke the guards became brutal and indifferent to the prisoners in the camps. They were continually reminded that inmates were the inferior but implacable enemies of Nazism.

BELOW: The journey to hell begins. Jews board a cattle train for transportation to Auschwitz concentration camp. At the other end they would be met by the inhuman camp doctor, SS-Hauptsturmführer Dr Josef Mengele. He would decide who would be put to slave labour and who would go to the gas chambers.

LEFT: The clothing workshop at Dachau. Here Jewish tailors sewed all kinds of uniforms and undertook the manufacture of SS insignia. Himmler planned to send the 'racially worthless' to concentration camps to learn 'obedience, diligence, unconditional subordination and loyalty towards the German masters. They must count up to 100, learn to recognise the traffic signs and be prepared for their trade as agricultural workers, fitters, stonemasons, carpenters, etc. The girls are to be trained as workers on the land, weavers, spinners, knitters and the like'.

RIGHT: A column of prisoners marches between the buildings at Dachau concentration camp under the watchful eye of their SS guards. The camp guards were taught that qualities such as charity and mercy were useless, outmoded absurdities.

LEFT: The stone quarry, in contrast to the clothing workshop illustrated above, was hell on earth. This is the quarry at Mauthausen concentration camp where, regardless of the weather conditions, prisoners weakened by malnutrition and beatings were forced to lift heavy stones up the 148 steps to waiting railway carts. Those who could not carry out the work for any reason were either shot or clubbed to death. All would eventually die, the only question was when, but the guards made sure that every ounce of labour was extracted before death came as a welcome release. Throughout the war there was a continual interchange of personnel between the Waffen-SS and the concentration camp guards. These transfers involved both officers and enlisted men, and give the lie to the notion that the Waffen-SS did not know of the genocide.

RIGHT: The last class photograph taken in Oradour-sur-Glane before elements of the *Das Reich* Division arrived in the village to exact revenge on the inhabitants for the deaths of several Waffen-SS soldiers at the hands of the Resistance. These girls were herded into the church, which was then set on fire, killing all of those inside. In all 642 people of both sexes and of all ages were murdered at Oradour, which was never rebuilt – a reminder of the inhuman side of the Waffen-SS.

BELOW: Concentration camp survivors at the end of the war. Despite their condition they are the lucky ones, unlike the millions who have been gassed and the hundreds of thousands who have been shot in eastern Europe. After his capture Himmler was shown pictures of of bodies at Buchenwald. He replied: 'Am I responsible for the excesses of my subordinates?'

ABOVE: Germans are shown their handiwork by their American captors after the end of the war. Ever since May 1945 the veterans of the Waffen-SS have sought to distance themselves from the atrocities committed in the name of National Socialism. But can a military force created in an ideological mould to be the standard bearer of Nazism ever succeed in such a venture? It is doubtful, for the reality is that, for all their valour and self-sacrifice on the battlefield, worthy and admirable though it was, there is a dark side to actions of Himmler's troops. The historian George Stein puts it thus: 'While neither SS ideological training materials nor Himmler's inspirational speeches need be accepted at face value as Waffen-SS beliefs in practice, it is true that the nihilism of the Waffen-SS was reinforced and given direction by National Socialist ideology ... When called upon, as individuals or units, to assist in such operations [atrocities] – whether it was the reduction of the Warsaw Ghetto or the extermination of Jews at Minsk – the men of the Waffen-SS displayed their cardinal virtue: blind obedience.' At the end of war the Waffen-SS took action even against German soldiers and civilians, shooting and hanging thousands for 'cowardice in the face of the enemy'. In

April 1945, for example, SS-Gruppenführer Max Simon, commander of the *Reichsführer-SS* Division, condemned an elderly farmer to death for disarming a group of Hitler Youth to prevent them being killed by approaching American forces. Even after Hitler's death fanatical Waffen-SS men continued to fight, for they had their oath of loyalty, bravery and 'obedience unto death'. This fanaticism had earned glory on the battlefield, but it could not be switched on and off like a tap. By 1945 it had become a religious creed, and woe betide anyone who interfered with it. The soldiers of the Waffen-SS had to be hardened to their task, as Himmler reminded the officers of the *Leibstandarte* in the autumn of 1940: 'Where, in temperatures of 40 degrees below zero we had to drag away thousands, tens of thousands, hundreds of thousand – where we had to have the hardness – you should listen to this, but forget it again at once – to shoot thousands of leading Poles, where we had to have the hardness, otherwise it would have rebounded on us later. In many cases it is much easier to go into battle with a company of infantry than it is to carry out executions or drag people away.' This hardness was the Waffen-SS's great strength; it was also responsible for horrendous atrocities.

INDEX